ONLY THE BRAVE

ALSO BY DON KEITH

ONLY THE BRAVE

July 1944–The Epic Battle for Guam

DON KEITH

CALIBER

CALIBER

An imprint of Penguin Random House LLC
penguinrandomhouse.com

DUTTON CALIBER and the CALIBER colophon are registered trademarks
of Penguin Random House LLC.

LIBRARY OF CONGRESS CATALOGING-IN-PUBLICATION DATA

Names: Keith, Don, 1947– author.
Title: Only the brave: July 1944—the epic battle for Guam / Don Keith.
Other titles: July 1944—the epic battle for Guam
Description: New York: Dutton Caliber [2021] | Series: [American War Heroes]
Identifiers: LCCN 2020053842 (print) | LCCN 2020053843 (ebook) |
ISBN 9780593184592 (paperback) | ISBN 9780593184608 (ebook)
Subjects: LCSH: World War, 1939–1945—Campaigns—Guam.
Classification: LCC D767.99.G8 K45 2021 (print) |
LCC D767.99.G8 (ebook) | DDC 940.54/2667—dc23
LC record available at https://lccn.loc.gov/2020053842
LC ebook record available at https://lccn.loc.gov/2020053843

Printed in the United States of America
1st Printing

For the people of Guam

★ CONTENTS ★

ONLY THE BRAVE

PROLOGUE

Carmen Artero was already excited on that bright and beautiful festival day, but the six-year-old was even more thrilled when she heard the throbbing drone of approaching airplane engines.

"Pan Am. Pan Am," she whispered to her sister, nine-year-old Maria. Both girls giggled, wishing they could run from the church plaza in time to maybe catch a glimpse of the big Boeing 314 Clipper "flying boat" as it came in low above Agaña, vectoring for a water landing down the coastline, near the town of Sumay, on Apra Harbor. The Pan Am plane was always such a majestic sight!

But they knew they could not go see it. Not this day. The girls had far more pressing obligations. And besides, the flying

1

boat certainly would be back in one week for its regularly scheduled arrival. It always was.

No, there was so much taking place on this, a special day of celebration on the island. It was December 8, falling this year on a Monday. And it was the day of the annual festival honoring Santa Marian Kamalen (Our Lady of Camarin, "Mary of the Crabs"), the patron saint of Guam. The sisters were only two among the scores of happy children who were part of the events at the cathedral and in the Plaza de España that morning. Many of them were dressed as angels, carrying baskets of flowers to strew along the streets of Agaña, the capital village.

Some of them were assigned to dance ahead of and beside the ancient wood-and-ivory statue of Santa Marian Kamalen as it was carried through town. The rendering had been carefully removed earlier in the day from its usual resting place, inside Dulce Nombre de Maria Cathedral-Basilica. Except for this event each December 8, she hung in a niche in the sanctuary wall behind the altar, just as she had done for more than three hundred years. The removal of the statue, the parade through the palm-lined streets of Agaña, the festival and feast—all were part of a tradition being carried out this day exactly as it had been for most of those three centuries.

It was important that the celebration be the best and most enthusiastic that it could be. Even little Carmen Artero knew it was crucial that she and the other children perform their jobs correctly to please not only their parents and islanders but also the priest and the saint herself. Afterward, they would have ample opportunity to enjoy the carnival atmosphere, the games with the other children, the wonderful food at the Feast of the

Immaculate Conception. But first they would lead those bearing the statue through the streets, among the thousands who had come to town for the day's events and to view the processional.

They had all heard the legends, handed down by word of mouth, from generation to generation, of the time when vandals swiped the statue. That was one of the occasions that the island had been ravaged by a typhoon that blew in shortly after the travesty. Santa Marian Kamalen protected Guam from typhoons, earthquakes, and tidal waves.

And, it was said, from war, too.

Carmen Artero and her sister managed to contain their excitement—and keep their homemade angel's wings straight—as Father Jesus Baza Dueñas said the rosary and prayed the novena in the beautiful plaza in front of the cathedral as a gentle breeze blew in from off the sea. Then, finally, the procession began, and the girls could put their nervous energy to good use.

The streets would be packed with people who had come from all parts of the island over the past few days. Some rode in their bull carts. Others came on foot. Many more drove. Some brought fresh fruits and vegetables to sell or share. More than a few slept in their carts or cars, or in the open air beneath lean-tos built with palm fronds under the tropical stars. Others stayed with friends and family. The excitement had been building, and now, with the sun climbing, it was palpable.

The procession had only moved a few blocks when Carmen once again heard the airplane engines, but they seemed to be farther away this time. Then there was another sound that could be heard, even above the crooning of the children. A sound like distant thunder.

Carmen walked on, though, singing a traditional hymn—"*A fragrant gift we give to you, our blessed mother*"—tossing flower petals, praying it would not rain and ruin her pretty dress and angel's wings. Her mother had worked so hard to make the outfit for her and she wanted nothing to spoil it.

Meanwhile, the family of another youngster, ten-year-old Antonio Palomo, was some distance away, trying to get closer to where the merrymaking was taking place. His parents had hoped to be able to take care of business in Sumay before heading for the celebration, a dozen miles farther up the coast. They were much later than they had hoped. The traffic on the highway for the Feast of the Immaculate Conception—85 percent of Guam's inhabitants were Catholic, but those of a different faith also enthusiastically participated—kept them from getting to the cathedral to take part in the rosary.

Instead, Antonio's father decided he would conduct the business some other day, park the car near Apra Harbor, and then try to find a spot along the processional route to at least catch a glimpse of the sacred statue as it was carried past. Antonio was disappointed but still excited, ready to join in the celebration and sample some of the delicious food they would have there.

Then, through his car window, he saw the approaching airplanes. Not a Pan Am flying boat at all. Smaller planes. He counted. Nine of them.

Americans! Perhaps flying overhead as part of the celebration, taking off from the several military airfields scattered around the island. The little boy felt a renewed swell of excitement in his chest. Despite the odd political attachment of his home island to the United States of America—one the boy did not at all understand—Guamanians were universally patriotic. They were proud to be a part of the United States, regardless of how far away across the Pacific Ocean that it might be from them.

Not citizens. "Nationals." But a part, nonetheless.

Just then, as he watched the planes get nearer, Antonio could see something falling from beneath them. Bombs?

What sort of salute is this? the boy asked himself. *Fireworks?*

The bombs exploded as they hit all around the Pan American Skyways Hotel and the Standard Oil tank farm on the hill nearby. Not far at all from his family's car. Antonio could feel the concussive blasts, smell the pungent aroma of something burning, and hear the shrieks of panic from the people closer to the hotel and along the roadway around them.

Then he heard the staccato noise of antiaircraft guns and spotted quick tracers zooming skyward from the U.S. Navy base in the distance. The boy quickly realized that this was not part of the festival.

As the aircraft pulled up and curved back out toward the sea, paralleling the shoreline of the peninsula, Antonio could clearly make out their distinctive markings. He could also hear the rattling of strafing machine guns, aimed at installations on the ground below the aircraft.

"Japanese! They are Japanese planes," his father muttered. "They have come."

Antonio's father had seen airplanes like these plenty of times before. He knew they were almost certainly flying from Japanese airfields on the island of Rota, only fifty miles north.

And from the bigger bases, also constructed by the Japanese on two of Guam's other sister islands in the Marianas chain, Tinian and Saipan. They were just over a hundred miles north. Those aircraft regularly passed over his home but never before at such low altitudes. They were usually much higher in the sky.

Now, all around them, islanders and military alike were stunned, panicked, running for whatever shelter they could find, even as the aircraft departed. Their car engine still humming, Antonio Palomo's father screeched away, headed back toward home. When they were once again on the highway, moving slowly to avoid people fleeing on foot, they drove past the navy yard at Piti, also near the bay. Buildings there were smoking, damaged, some still afire.

This was a bad, bad dream, Antonio thought as he took in the chaotic scene unfolding around him.

Like many others on Guam, his father had spoken of the possibilities of war between the United States and the Empire of Japan. But he believed that even if there should be war between the two powerful nations, Guam, barely on the periphery, would be spared. To most of the world, Guam was little more than a forgotten mound of volcanic rock lost in the warm waters of an exceptionally large ocean.

Besides, even if the Japanese did see strategic value in the island, neither they nor any other country would dare challenge the almighty United States of America. Not for this bit of out-of-the-way territory. Also, judging by the native Japanese population on Guam, many of whom had been on the island for generations, everyone knew them to be quiet, friendly, nice people, not at all threatening.

Even if they did suddenly decide to invade, why would the Japanese even bother to bomb the island? There was no need. If they wanted to take Guam, they could simply walk in, run a flag up the flagpole, and claim it, almost certainly without firing a shot.

Not far away, twenty-one-year-old U.S. Marine Corps private first class Ray Church was trying to get some rest before going back on duty. He had already been busy the last few weeks helping the others in the contingent that had been assigned to guard the Government House in Agaña—the headquarters for the U.S. Navy's commander and governor of the island—and also completing a rather ominous task. They had been busily bundling up and burning any documents that might be of military value should the Japanese suddenly remember that Guam was there. Just in case the Japanese decided to complete their collection of glittering tropical islands by adding the final jewel of the necklace that formed the Mariana Islands.

The Government House had been built by the Spanish in 1885 to replace a previous structure and had been called the "Governor's Palace" since the 1700s. It was an impressive stone building with a cantilevered balcony and clay tile roof. When the Americans moved in in 1898, they not only began calling the structure "the Government House" but also made other changes. Weapons storerooms on the first floor were converted to administrative offices. A reception area was added to the second floor, and there was also a dining room and the private residence of the military governor and his family. Kitchen facilities and quarters for servants and Marine guards were located at the rear. It was an impressive structure and the people of Guam were proud of it.

PFC Church was born in Henrieville, Utah, a pastoral farming area an hour southwest of Salt Lake City. After high school, he went to Dixie Junior College in St. George, Utah. Unable to afford to attend full-time and facing the draft, he enlisted in the Marines instead. After eleven weeks of basic training, he saw a request for volunteers to go to Guam, although he would later admit he had no idea where it was located. Once there, he volunteered again, this time to serve on the unit whose duty was to guard the governor's office in Agaña.

Church later remembered the "special training" he received for the post. "I followed the governor around and did whatever he wanted me to do," he related.

Indeed, it had been relatively easy duty for him ever since he had arrived on Guam the previous year. He found the place to be a mostly sleepy outpost reminiscent of his isolated little hometown back in Utah. The Chamorro people—inhabitants of the island for more than 4,000 years—were friendly and easygoing, not all that different in most ways from folks back home, although their Catholic religion was not exactly familiar to the young Marine. Church was a devout Mormon. But the people of Guam certainly seemed happy to have the Marines there. The weather was exceptional most of the year, except for the rainy season. It was certainly a warmer winter there than it was back in Utah. The guard duty at the governor's residence was not all that challenging, either. His fellow guards were a great bunch of guys. The natives of Guam who also served as Government House guards seemed to be a good group. His detachment shared the same cook as the governor and his staff, so they ate well. And he and the other seven Marines with whom he served had their own apartments, not barracks.

As far as the possibilities of war, few people whom Church spoke with really believed there would be an invasion by the Japanese, even if the oft-predicted war between the United States and the Empire of Japan should come about—even if military dependents and civilian personnel had already been evacuated, indicating that somebody higher up was convinced Guam might become involved if there were a conflict.

Church believed, as many Guamanians did, that the Japanese would see no more value in their island—despite its size and location—than the U.S. government and military had. So the private could only wonder where else in the Pacific he might be sent to fight if Guam was not invaded.

Now, though, all speculation about the possibility of war between the United States and Japan had come to an abrupt and ominous end. It was no longer conjecture.

Church and his fellow Marines and sailors would soon learn the catastrophic news—news that would greatly escalate the likelihood that their outpost in paradise would soon be a part of something far bigger and deadlier.

At 0445 on the morning of the festival of Santa Marian Kamalen—Monday, December 8, 1941—Captain George McMillin had been awakened with a disturbing report. He was the overall commander of the Marine and Navy garrison on Guam. But also, by law, he was the island's governor. He was informed that the Japanese had launched a sudden attack on naval facilities at Pearl Harbor, in Hawaii. Since Hawaii was on the other side of the international date line, it was still Sunday, December 7, over there.

McMillin was not totally surprised, but he was deeply concerned about his many friends at Pearl. The one and only ship he had ever commanded, the repair vessel USS *Medusa* (AR-1), was now based there, with most of his old crew still aboard. (McMillin would learn much later that his former repair ship and crew not only survived intact but struck some blows of their own during the attack, helping track and sink a Japanese mini-submarine and shooting down two of the attackers' Aichi D3A1 dive-bombers.)

But that was not the only shocking news flash that day. In addition to the stunning assault on Pearl Harbor, Japanese bombers would also hit U.S. bases in the Philippines ten hours later. And that was a mere 1,500 miles to the west of Guam.

Damage and casualties were reported to be extreme there as well. Adding to the surprise of the assault on the Philippines was the fact that General Douglas MacArthur, the head of the U.S. Army in the Far East at the time, had declared Manila to be an open city. That meant that it would be mostly undefended. That fact had not deterred the Empire of Japan.

Although there was no official declaration yet, McMillin made the assumption that America was now almost certainly at war—with a country that had constructed major military facilities only a short distance away from Guam, on sister islands within the Mariana chain. There was also a vast area of South Pacific islands—termed "Japanese mandates" and under officially sanctioned control of the Empire—located to the east and south of the dollop of land McMillin oversaw. Those other islands in a vast ocean virtually surrounded Guam, which had so far been little more than a forgotten U.S. territory—one that, by 1941, was also a very isolated one.

Private Ray Church was in his quarters that morning when he heard a commotion in the streets. Locals were scrambling about and told him there had been aircraft flying over, dropping bombs, and there was damage, many injuries, and deaths.

Church promptly got dressed even though he was scheduled to be off duty that day. He learned there had been air attacks at other points along the western side of the island—primarily at the town of Sumay, near the location of the Navy base—and that the Japanese had also bombed Pearl Harbor.

As he carried out his preassigned duties and began to prepare barricades around the Government House, Church thought about some of the things that he had observed recently—signs that now made plenty more sense to him. An increased number of Japanese aircraft, flying at higher altitude up and down the shoreline. Impressions in the wet sand along the beach that he had recognized as something likely made by the flippers of frogmen.

As he and his fellow Marines worked furiously, more details came in about the air attack that morning on the Marine barracks and other targets on the island, locations only about a dozen miles down the island's western coast from Agaña. And then the planes—a grand total of nine of them breaking formation as they swooped in—came roaring back, this time bombing Agaña itself, mere blocks from the Government House, not far from where the Feast of the Immaculate Conception procession was supposed to be taking place.

Church could only wonder what their chances were if the Japanese did invade Guam. His detachment's orders were clear: he was to defend the governor and the Government House. But if there should be a Japanese invasion, the odds of them being able to successfully do so were slim to none.

Private Church hunkered down, cached his ammunition, and cinched up his helmet chin strap, ready to do what he had vowed to do: "support and defend the Constitution of the United States against all enemies, foreign and domestic . . . obey the orders of the officers appointed over me." Every American warrior had taken the same oath.

U.S. Navy radioman first class George Tweed had first come to Guam in 1939, dreading duty in such a sleepy, out-of-the-way place on the other side of the world from his native Oregon. He had quickly come to love everything about the island. He had been surprised by how cosmopolitan the towns were, with roads, cars, and all the modern conveniences. How pleasant the people were, too. Chamorros—native islanders who preferred to be called "Guamanians"—made up just about the entire population. Of the 23,000 people there, about 22,000 were Chamorro. The rest of the non-natives were Japanese, Chinese, and American. Most spoke the Chamorro language at home instead of the official language, English.

But Tweed was equally surprised by how much of the island was virtually deserted and difficult to traverse. He speculated there were plenty of areas in the thick, mountainous jungles on both ends of the human-foot-shaped isle that had likely never been explored. When he was off duty, and especially after his wife and two sons were exiled back to the States the previous October, he enjoyed hiking remote parts of the island alone, over tall volcanic mountains, through thick jungle, along the high cliffs overlooking the sea. He was particularly impressed with Mount Lamlam—"lightning" in the language of the Chamorros—a crest that the islanders proudly proclaimed to be the highest peak on planet Earth. Though its highest point is only about 1,300 feet above sea level, it slopes continuously downward from Guam's southwest coastline near the town of Agat, plunging into the sea, and then progresses all the way to the bottom of the Mariana Trench, which is more than 36,000 feet deep. From that perspective, Lamlam is more than 8,000 feet taller than Mount Everest.

Tweed enjoyed his work in the Navy communications office, too. There he not only received and sent radio messages but was also responsible for keeping the radios and antennas working properly. That, and assure that there was an adequate supply of parts to repair them and keep them in service. Tweed was especially proud that his group was the primary source of news from the rest of the world, not only for his fellow military personnel, but also the good people of Guam. Communications were crucial way out there, and Tweed was one of the men primarily charged with keeping things working.

Early on December 8, when word of the Pearl Harbor assault came in, Tweed was awakened and promptly drove over to the communications office. When he asked the chief on duty what they were supposed to do now that an invasion appeared more likely, he was told, "I don't know."

In his long tour of duty on Guam, Tweed, too, had noticed with concern how ill-prepared and seemingly overlooked the sailors and Marines there were. It quickly became even more of a worry later that morning when the bombs began falling and the strafing started. Tweed immediately found work to do. The enemy planes had destroyed telephone lines atop Libugon Hill, overlooking the town of Agaña and Agaña Bay. He rushed up there with a radio transmitter to use while he tried to fix the mess.

Planes flew in, and he was strafed. He even had a bomb dropped in his general area as he worked. He wondered why the Japanese were wasting so much effort and ordnance on a single sailor until he realized they were more likely aiming at an aircraft beacon tower on a nearby ridge. Then, when he got back home, he discovered that the only bomb the Japanese dropped on the little town where he lived had destroyed his house.

Of course, Tweed had no idea that an ordeal of two years and seven months of constantly dodging the Japanese was just beginning for him. Or that his would be yet another remarkable story among the many that would emerge from the two battles for the island of Guam.

While the island residents likely had no real concept of what was about to happen, Church, Tweed, and their fellow sailors and Marines knew only too well what this sudden air attack meant. It was merely a prelude. The likelihood of a Japanese invasion was now much more probable. The Japanese would not drop bombs or strafe the island if they did not see some value in Guam. Nor would they waste the ordnance if they did not intend to follow up with an incursion.

Also, McMillin, Church, Tweed, and the rest of the Marines and sailors on the island of Guam were aware of another troubling fact—something the gentle Guamanians, most of whom were not yet born the last time their island had been invaded by a foreign force, likely did not know.

The U.S. military and the island's own defensive forces were pitifully prepared to do anything to stop what was about to happen.

number of swift outrigger canoes that raced out from the

CHAPTER ONE

THE ISLAND OF THE THIEVES

When the Portuguese explorer Ferdinand Magellan and his crew landed on what is now the island of Guam on March 6, 1521, they were most impressed by the vast number of swift outrigger canoes that raced out from the shoreline to meet them. The boats seemed to fly across the water, leading Magellan to immediately name the place Islas de las Velas Latinas (Islands of the Lateen Sails). The welcoming inhabitants seemed friendly enough. Even better, they brought with them fresh fruit and vegetables for trade. After a long, stormy, and deadly voyage, that was exactly what the explorer and the crew members of his three remaining vessels needed. Many of them suffered from scurvy and malnutrition.

But Magellan soon decided to make his stop at this place a brief one. Crewmen reported the locals had helped themselves to whatever they wanted from the ships. Even a small boat had been swiped from the deck of the flagship. The native Chamorro people simply assumed this was how the trade process was supposed to work. Magellan disagreed. He dispatched a party ashore to recover whatever they could. Then they sailed on.

Magellan did not even take time to claim the island for Spain, on whose behalf he had launched this mission, or to attempt to force the natives to convert to Christianity, as was his usual practice. That was a bit of good luck for the Chamorros. Magellan typically accomplished both goals by violent means if the indigenous peoples objected even the slightest. As they hastily left the island behind and sailed westward, his men did rename the place Islas de los Ladrones (Islands of the Thieves).

Magellan's primary mission was to prove a western sea route existed from Spain to the Molucca Islands, the so-called Spice Islands. He also was bound to prove that he could circumnavigate the globe as part of the mission. By finding the course around Cabo de Hornos (Cape Horn), the southern point of what is now the South American continent, they were well on their way to demonstrating a navigational feat that many in Europe considered suicidal.

Yet, by this point in the ambitious voyage, some of Magellan's crew members had grown weary and were on the brink of mutiny. Some already had left, turning back, and taking two ships with them. And it would be only six weeks after his brief visit to the Islands of the Thieves that Magellan would die in a battle in what is now the Philippines. That would come while he was attempting to coerce a group there to accept allegiance to Spain and the Christian god. The natives there were decidedly and violently unwilling to do either.

Magellan's demise convinced more members of his crew it was time to quit the expedition. They took two more ships with them. Eventually a few remaining sailors—and a single ship of the original five—would reach the Spice Islands and then, from there, complete the voyage around the world, returning to Spain. Although Magellan would be credited with circumnavigating the globe, he was in reality denied the opportunity to successfully complete the voyage.

The remote island of Guam would be mostly overlooked for a good part of the next half century. Then it was another explorer, one less well-known, who came along and claimed it and her sister islands for Spain in 1565. As one of the larger spots of land in the region, and despite the numerous dangerous reefs and inaccessible cliffs, General Miguel López de Legazpi recognized the value of the place as a stopover for the galleons that were by then plying the trade routes—some of which had been established by Magellan and his crew—from the Philippines to western Mexico. Defensive fortifications, some of which are still visible today, were constructed on Guam by Legazpi and his men, but not before skirmishes with the Chamorros, who were still not sure about these white-skinned interlopers and their threats to the island's traditions. Especially when the Spanish sailors burned some native huts to show their intent to rule. It would be only three years later when the first Catholic church was built on Guam.

Legazpi went on to the Philippines—already named for the

Spanish king Philip II—where he established the capital city of Cebu, from which he hoped to administer what he had dubbed on his maps the Spanish East Indies. That included little more than the Philippines and the Mariana Islands. Even though opposition to the Spanish continued, the natives of the region eventually relented. Like his predecessor, Magellan, Legazpi did not live to see the completion of his quest. Before he had brought Catholicism and Spanish colonization to all areas of the Spanish East Indies, he died one day in 1572 while vehemently reprimanding an aide.

The following three and a half centuries were not easy for Guam, as they were marked by typhoons, earthquakes, tsunamis, epidemics, and sporadic hostilities between the Spanish colonists and Chamorro rebels. The people who eventually became Chamorros were a branch of the Filipino people. They had populated what were eventually named the Mariana Islands about two thousand years before Christ. They understandably did not want to give up their way of life, sovereignty, or long-held religious beliefs. Even so, Guam and the rest of the Marianas would remain under the control of Spain for more than three hundred years after Magellan and Legazpi.

Spain certainly recognized their value. Especially that of Guam, which is the largest island in the Mariana chain, thirty miles long from north to south and varying from four to twelve miles wide, with 212 square miles of territory consisting mostly of volcanically formed mountains and thick jungle. But that was not why Spain coveted the island. It also has a reasonably good natural harbor at Apra. And it had risen from the sea in an almost perfect location to fit the needs of the Spanish.

Guam is strategically located in the Pacific Ocean amid the scattered islands of the Micronesia subregion. With the Philippines to the west and North and South America to the east, and with Guam as a convenient stopover along the way, the Spanish had finally and effectively created the trans-Pacific Manila galleon trade route they had long imagined. Silver that was mined in Mexico and what is now Bolivia could be exchanged for silk, porcelain, spices, gems, and other goods highly valued by Europeans. Those goods were available in abundance in the Spice Islands, the Moluccas (now the Maluku Islands), in eastern Indonesia and west of New Guinea. But most importantly for Spain, the commerce that passed through Guam helped finance the growing Spanish Empire. That only magnified the importance of Guam and its neighbors.

Even so, to most of the world, Guam remained forgotten, a bit of spiky, vegetation-covered ground amid many more bits of similar dry land arrayed like intentionally placed stepping-stones across a vast ocean.

Very few Americans, then or today, could pinpoint the island on a map when Guam suddenly became a U.S. territory in 1898. Nor could they have explained how such a thing came about. Most of them would have been better able to locate the Philippines, Cuba, or Puerto Rico, all of which were also ceded to the United States the same way as Guam was. They were lumped into the Treaty of Paris, which ended the Spanish-American War. That same treaty also effectively wiped out one of the most powerful and far-flung empires in the history of the planet, that of Spain.

Each one of the entities ceded to the United States by the

treaty would have a different fate. Cuba, a mere ninety miles from the U.S. mainland, was granted its independence in 1902. The Philippines would still technically be a part of the United States when World War II started and would not receive their full sovereignty until 1946. Puerto Rico remains an "unincorporated territory of the United States" to this day.

The status of Guam and its inhabitants has changed only marginally since the Treaty of Paris. The island officially fell under control of the U.S. Navy when President William McKinley signed an executive order on December 23, 1898. Guamanians were mostly happy to be a part of America, even if, once the dust settled, their northern sister islands in the Mariana chain ended up belonging to, of all places, Germany.

The newly arrived Americans made quick work of establishing a naval shipyard on the western side of the island at the town of Piti, on Apra Harbor. They also constructed a barracks for Marines at Sumay, a town on Guam's Orote Peninsula, the land that juts out into the sea just south of Piti. They were built there to protect the new U.S. possession, because more ambitious plans were being made to convert the island into a major naval facility at the far side of the Pacific. Many in Congress and the Navy felt such a base was crucial. Just as the early Spanish explorers had, the U.S. Navy saw great value and wonderful possibilities for Guam.

Captain Richard P. Leary, a naval officer who had seen action in both the American Civil War and the Spanish-American War, was designated as governor of Guam. He would also serve as commandant for the naval base. Leary would be the first of an eventual thirty-eight different military governors who would oversee the island for the next forty-three years. Few stayed for more than about a year. Such a position was not considered to be beneficial for career advancement.

On August 7, 1899, the U.S. Naval Station on Guam was formally established. But it did not include just the area around Apra Harbor; the naval station would consist of the entire island. Locals would have no say in the matter. Even if they lived on family land that had been theirs for generations, it now technically belonged to the U.S. Navy. This policy was later modified, although the military and its need for land would become a point of contention that continues to this day.

As the world entered the twentieth century, and after the quick victory in the Spanish-American War, it appeared Guam was well on its way to becoming the major naval facility for the United States that so many had coveted.

It was a prospect that failed to pan out. The U.S. Navy eventually decided to develop Pearl Harbor, on the Hawaiian island of Oahu, as its main base in the Pacific Ocean and not the island of Guam. That was because Pearl was located much closer to the mainland and, in the opinion of those who mattered, offered a better natural harbor.

As a token gesture, a half dozen six-inch guns were emplaced on Guam, and there were other plans to build up the island's defenses. In reality, though, nothing much happened. Not even before and after World War I, when some in the military touted the same strategic value in protecting the shipping routes to and from the Philippines that the Spanish had recognized centuries earlier.

There was plenty swapping of ownership going on among

all the other islands in the region during this time. That included Guam's sister islands in the Marianas. In 1899, Germany charged in and purchased from Spain the other fourteen volcanic islands in the chain, which form a crescent-shaped line marking the eastern edge of the Philippine Sea. They also bought the Marshall Islands and the Caroline Islands, which lay to the south and east of Guam.

Then, in 1914, just after the start of World War I, Japan seized all those from Germany. In 1920, the League of Nations generously gave Japan a legal mandate to govern all of the former German possessions in the South Pacific. All that territory was designated as Japanese mandates. Without hesitation, the Japanese Empire immediately began colonizing and exploiting economically that wide swath of tropical Pacific territory. The emperor had already realized that his nation's desired recognition as a major world power and its efforts to colonize and control territories around the globe depended not only on the land but the natural resources they contained. And now, with the full approval of the members of the League of Nations, Japan had legal control over both, from just south of the Home Islands almost all the way to Australia.

The United States had already begun to worry about this situation in the Pacific, especially as it related to the Philippines and Guam. America took a hard line at the Washington Naval Conference in 1921–22. The result was a sweeping agreement between Japan and the United States that neither country would make any moves to fortify militarily any of their possessions in the western Pacific. For the United States, that only included the Philippines and Guam. And the agreement assured that no further effort would be undertaken to put that long-planned major naval base on Guam. Or to do anything else to protect the island. Even the six-inch guns that had been placed there were dismantled and removed in 1930. The Americans took the term "not fortify militarily" quite seriously.

Meanwhile, Japan went the other direction. They proceeded to build up what they termed "defensive" military facilities on many of their possessions in the region. That included the islands of Saipan and Tinian in the Marianas.

Some still wondered why the United States was not taking advantage of the strategic location Guam offered. Even as late as 1939, there remained talk in the higher circles of the Navy of putting an advanced naval fleet base there, but nothing happened. Instead, just the opposite occurred.

Early in 1941, Guam was given a "category F" defense rating. The whole world knew it, including Japan. In practical terms, that meant nothing new was to be done to prepare to defend the island against attack or invasion. Should there be an impending assault, naval and Marine forces based there would be ordered to destroy facilities and records to prevent them from falling into enemy hands. Then they were to get the hell out of Dodge!

Only later did the reasoning for the category F designation become clearer. Key members of Congress—especially those who wanted to avoid war at all costs, both in the Pacific and Europe, after having been reluctantly dragged into World War I— were concerned that any effort to put defenses on Guam might antagonize the Japanese. That could be just enough to provoke them into some kind of retaliation, one sufficient to ignite the dreaded bonfire of a multifront war. This logic was reinforced when Japan, Italy, and Germany signed the Tripartite Pact in September 1940 under which the three governments united "for the purpose of realizing their ultimate object, world peace"—but making it clear that war with any one of them was war with all three of them.

The Japanese would easily have observed any U.S. military buildup on Guam. They would not have ignored such a "non-defensive" act. After all, Japan had an air base on the small island of Rota, just about fifty miles north of Ritidian Point, on Guam's northern tip. They regularly overflew the island with aircraft based there. And although forbidden to do so by the agreement they had signed in 1922, the Japanese Empire had constructed even more impressive facilities farther north on Tinian and Saipan. Those islands were located less than 130 miles away from American soil on Guam, also a short flight.

With tensions between America and Japan so high, there was still hope that war would be averted. The United States continued to help allies in Europe in the face of Hitler's advances but had so far avoided joining that conflict. Many, including President Franklin Roosevelt, felt that a world war was not necessarily inevitable and should be avoided.

There is some irony in the fact that in November of 1941, Japanese envoy Saburo Kurusu, appointed by his prime minister, Hideki Tojo, made a stop on Guam. He was on his way to Washington, D.C., with diplomatic papers in his pouch that were part of continuing negotiations between the nations. Talks that both Tokyo and Washington hoped would ease tensions and avoid war. The Pan American Clipper on which Kurusu flew made its usual stop in Guam, easing down for a water landing in Apra Harbor. The envoy was seen stepping off the plane, the diplomatic pouch in hand, for a break during the layover. It would be only a month later when far more of his countrymen trod the soil of Guam.

Many on the island saw Kurusu's brief visit as a good omen. It was not. Ultimately, it was Kurusu who delivered the Japanese ultimatum to U.S. officials in Washington, D.C., even as the Empire's aircraft carriers, decks loaded with bombers and torpedo planes, were on their way to wreak havoc on Pearl Harbor in a less diplomatic attempt to prevent America from entering the war.

By then, Captain George Johnson McMillin—a native of Youngstown, Ohio, a graduate of the U.S. Naval Academy, a veteran of World War I, the occupation of the Dominican Republic, and the occupation of Veracruz—had become the thirty-eighth (and, as it turned out, final) U.S. military governor of the island of Guam. That also made him commander of Naval Forces, Guam, Asiatic Fleet. He started his new job in April of 1940.

McMillin had already faced a serious problem early in his administration. A monstrous typhoon with winds exceeding 125 miles per hour struck the island in November of 1940, part of a historically active storm season in that part of the world. Practically every building on the island suffered damage, including the Pan American Hotel and a hangar at the airfield. Five islanders died. Now, just over a year later, with the nation possibly on the brink of war, he faced a far more daunting challenge. He might need to defend Guam against the powerful

Japanese war machine with only 547 Marines and sailors, including four Navy nurses, and just a few vessels.

One of those vessels, the station ship USS *Gold Star* (AG-12), was not even in port at the time. She and her crew of 137 men had steamed the 1,500 miles to the Philippines on a resupply mission. And while they were there, the men intended to do some Christmas shopping. But there were sufficient rumblings that the Navy asked Captain McMillin to order the *Gold Star* to remain in the Philippines for a while. Christmas would have to come late for many that year.

There were 153 Marines at the barracks at Sumay, armed only with a few machine guns, Browning automatic rifles (BARs), and Springfield rifles. The Marines advised three separate Guamanian units. The Guam Insular Patrol, consisting of about eighty men, was, in effect, the island's police force, armed with .38-caliber pistols, and dispersed around the island in towns and villages. The Guam Militia was no more than a ceremonial unit and was not armed at all. The main defense force was the Guam Insular Force Guard, consisting of about 250 men at the beginning of December 1941. That number had been doubled earlier in the year as one of the few noticeable preparations for trouble. And that total included sixteen men who were only trained as members of a marching band. The rest were armed with seven machine guns, a few pistols, and about eighty-five Springfield rifles. Several men who were there remember that many of the rifles carried labels on their stocks that said, "Do not fire. For training purposes only." They also recall that many of the guard—including most of the new recruits—had never fired a gun, not even for target practice.

With the *Gold Star* gone, the only "warship" McMillin had at his disposal was the minesweeper USS *Penguin* (AM-33), fittingly nicknamed "Old Duck," since she had been laid down way back in November of 1917. Early on the morning of December 8, the *Penguin* returned from a short patrol around the island to deliver supplies to towns and villages. They dropped anchor in Apra Harbor near the other naval facilities. When word came of the attack on Pearl Harbor, the crew was ordered to remain aboard, just in case. But that message had to be delivered by motor launch because the minesweeper's radio was not working.

The ship's captain immediately ordered the flag to be flown upside down, "a signal of dire distress in instances of extreme danger to life or property," according to the United States Flag Code. Still, most of the crew had doubts that anyone would actually attack the island. Or their ship.

Captain McMillin, clearly aware of his defensive limitations, could only hope that the Japanese had too many other targets to go after, that they had made their point with the attack on Pearl Harbor, and they would see little value in taking Guam. Even so, when he was awakened with the news of the attack in Hawaii, he referred to a prepared list of things to do and began to get ready for the worst-case scenario.

He ordered that certain groups of civilian Guamanians be evacuated, primarily those in or near what he felt would be likely military targets. The civil population had been previously instructed about what they should do during air raids. That mostly meant going to the ranches of friends or families deeper into the island, away from the principal towns and military installations. American civilians—mostly dependents of military men stationed there and employees of Pan Am and Standard Oil—had all been sent to Hawaii or the U.S. mainland back in October 1940. That included the family of Captain McMillin: his wife, Annabel; his sixteen-year-old daughter, Anne; and his fourteen-year-old son George Jr.

McMillin had also ordered a contingent of the Marines to immediately begin rounding up and jailing Japanese nationals living on the island. All navigation lights were ordered extinguished. Finally, he commanded that schools, the Bank of Guam, and churches be closed until further notice. That was probably not necessary. It was the day of the Feast of the Immaculate Conception, the island's biggest holiday, and most schools and business establishments would be shut down anyway.

When considering his assets, McMillin certainly had confidence in the Marine contingent down at Sumay. Their commander, Lieutenant Colonel William K. MacNulty, had trained them well on what they might do to defend the island, should it ever come to that. MacNulty was already a decorated hero with the demonstrated ability to get the most from his men. The Pennsylvania native had received the Silver Star for gallantry at the Battle of the Argonne Forest during World War I and the Navy Cross for action in the Second Nicaraguan Campaign in 1928.

The citation for the Navy Cross described how MacNulty, then a Marine captain, responded to a situation not unlike the one he might soon face on Guam: "Upon receiving word that a platoon of the 57th Company had been ambushed by a numerically superior force, [he] immediately upon his own initiative proceeded to the scene, made a night march over unknown, most difficult terrain, in a bandit-infested area. Upon arrival at the spot, Captain MacNulty disposed his patrol with such military ability and strategy as to successfully defeat and put to rout the bandit force, thereby saving the lives of the remaining few of the beleaguered patrol, which were at that time greatly outnumbered."

Certainly, Lieutenant Colonel William MacNulty was one tough-nut Marine, proven able to do the most with whatever assets he had.

McMillin was also confident that Guam's Insular Guard, despite their lack of training and weapons, would do the best they could, just as their Chamorro ancestors had done against the Spanish and other aggressors over thousands of years. He knew they would not willingly allow anyone else to invade their island.

But the captain had to be aware that the Japanese possessed far superior forces and long-established bases nearby from which to sortie. They had many capable warplanes only a hop, a skip, and a jump away.

Still, Captain McMillin had already made the decision to defend the island the best they could. Only the brave could harbor a hope, but it was their duty. It was why they were billeted there on Guam. It was what they had trained for. And, by God, they would do everything they could.

Then, at 8:47 a.m. Guam time, the first Japanese bomb fell on the Piti navy yard in Sumay. The air assault would last two days but with never more than nine aircraft attacking at a time, and only during the daytime.

Then, before sunrise on December 10, the First Battle of

Guam began with the Japanese invasion of the Island of the Thieves, then ended very quickly with the inevitable surrender by Captain McMillin to the invasion force commander. It would require, from start to finish, less than four hours.

For the first time since the War of 1812, American soil would be invaded and captured by a foreign enemy. And the entire thing would take about the same amount of time as the annual jubilant processional through the streets of Agaña in honor of Mary of the Crabs and the Feast of the Immaculate Conception.

CHAPTER TWO

"THE NEW ORDER OF THE WORLD"

The Japanese invasion of Guam was just a minor part of a much larger thrust code-named "Operation Z." On December 8, 1941, on the western side of the international date line, bombing would begin not only on the southernmost island of the Marianas but also Malaya, the Philippines, Borneo, Java, and Wake Island. In several of these places, including the island of Guam, the plan was to land assault forces within days or weeks of the initial air assaults.

When the first Imperial Japanese Navy aircraft zoomed in over the harbor of Apra and began their attack, the crew of the *Penguin*, which had been anchored and waiting for whatever might happen, quickly slipped her moorings and moved out beyond the point at the end of the Orote Peninsula to allow for maneuvering. They manned guns and began firing back. That immediately made the minesweeper an even more obvious target. In minutes the ship was damaged and likely sinking. To keep the vessel from falling into enemy hands, the crew went ahead and scuttled her in deeper water. One officer who was manning one of the ship's guns was killed—Ensign Robert White, likely the first death in the Battle of Guam—and several other men, including the captain, were injured. The crewmen either swam or rowed to shore in lifeboats between attacks.

One crew member on the *Penguin*, Edward Howard, later recalled watching the ship sink as they made for shore. "The last thing that went down was the American flag. It was like a fantasy world. This isn't happening. This couldn't happen. It was just unreal."

As with many of the men off the *Penguin* and those digging in to defend the island, Edward Howard had no idea of the long ordeal he was beginning. In his case, the invasion would cost him not only his freedom but also the life of his wife. And the suffering and its effects would linger with him for another fifty years.

Meanwhile, the attacking Japanese aircraft strafed the oil depot ship *Robert L. Barnes* (AO-14). She soon began taking on water. Her crew was unable to intentionally sink their ship because she had been immobile for some time, already resting in shallow water.

From the decks of both vessels, men could see smoke and fire all around the small harbor. The Standard Oil tank farm was ablaze. The Marine barracks and navy yard at Piti were smoking. The radio station at Libugon had been destroyed and was now silent. Even the Pan American Hotel was on fire. Two Chamorro kitchen workers died there.

Two older yard patrol boats, the *YP-16* and *YP-17*, were the only other naval vessels in the harbor at the time. The *YP-16* was set afire and sunk by her crew. The *YP-17* would later be captured and used by the Japanese.

Back at the cathedral on the Plaza de España, Carmen Artero and her sister noticed that the priest had stopped before he had even started to say the mass. Someone was whispering something in his ear. Then, with a pained look on his face, he told everyone to run, run home, run and find their families. The island was under attack!

Everyone began shrieking, crying, in a panic. Carmen and Maria darted all about, looking and calling for their father, Antonio Artero, who had brought them to the plaza that morning. Artero owned a market in Agaña where he sold meat from animals raised on his family's farm elsewhere on the island. But the girls could not find him amid the chaotic, terrified crowd.

Then Carmen spotted their mother and aunt and the girls ran to them. As soon as they did, a plane plunged low, roaring overhead. They all dove beneath a house until the plane was gone. Carmen later related that she landed on a turtle beneath the house and was afraid she may have hurt it. That at least took her mind off the danger they were in. Once the planes were gone, they took a bus home, still wondering where Carmen's father might be. Their joyous festival day had turned to one of terror and uncertainty.

The raids by the Japanese aircraft continued most of the day, until about 5:00 p.m. local time. Then they abruptly ceased.

Everyone on the island waited nervously for the drone of another airplane engine, for the next explosion, for ships to appear on the horizon and the invasion to begin. Captain McMillin sent word to all the island's inhabitants to find shelter, that more destruction was likely on the way. Many Chamorros left towns and villages to go to the ranches (actually, more like farms) of relatives or friends. Before the war, few people lived at their ranches. They stayed in the towns and went to the ranches to care for animals and crops. That changed during those first few days in December 1941. For example, young Antonio Palomo and most of his family fled to his maternal grandparents' ranch inland. They would spend most of the next two years there.

Meanwhile, Carmen Artero's father, who had looked for his wife and children in the crowded, tumultuous streets, finally found them at home. He put them into his automobile and attempted to drive them through Agaña to their family ranch on the northern end of the island. Frightened people tried to cling to or jump onto the car, begging, screaming, "Take us with you!"

Carmen remembers seeing her father get out, punching and pulling away from their car those who were impeding their progress. Then he would drive a few feet farther, only to be surrounded by more panicked townspeople, all desperate to get away from the loud, diving airplanes. She had never seen her father do such violent things, and she was stunned.

"It was the most shocking thing I have ever seen in my whole life," Artero later remembered. "The whole day was nothing but shock."

But the only invasion that landed the night of December 8

was by a group of nine Saipan natives who came ashore at about midnight at Ritidian Point. Three of them were captured by the Insular Patrol and brought to the Government House for interrogation. The insurgents gave little information other than that the Japanese would come ashore the next day, and the small group had been threatened with death for them and their families if they did not go ashore on Guam's northernmost point. They had been ordered to determine if there were any armaments or barricades there that might impede a landing.

Captain McMillin was incredulous. He assumed this was a diversion, attempting to get him to send his Marines to the north end of the island to repel an attack there rather than keep most of them near Sumay. That was where the bulk of the U.S. Navy facilities were and would almost certainly be the target of any invasion troops. He jailed the three intruders along with about fifty Japanese nationals, most of them longtime Guam residents. The few prisoners who had been in the jails had been released shortly after the first bombs fell and told to go home.

Beginning at about the same time as the day before, bombs once again rained down on Guam on Tuesday morning—always from nine airplanes in each wave—on some of the same targets as the previous day. There were attempts to bomb the Government House, in the heart of Agaña, but none hit home. The Japanese pilots also strafed villages, seemingly at random, resulting in civilian deaths and injuries as well as considerable damage. And, of course, even more panic.

Reports claimed that Japanese aircraft had been shot down,

including by sailors on the *Penguin* the first day of the attacks. That was not true. None of the reports were.

Captain McMillin received a communication from the Japanese on the second day of the air attacks, assuring him the island was surrounded and would be invaded if he did not surrender. McMillin replied that he would not.

Since Captain McMillin had already made the decision to prepare to defend the island against an invasion, the Marines were up and busy when the second day's bombing started. They were digging in near the rifle range on Orote Peninsula, which formed the southern part of Apra Harbor. They had help from about fifty crewmen from the *Penguin*.

The Guam Insular Force Guard secured government buildings in Agaña, assisting the Marines assigned to protect the commander/governor at the Government House. Again, everyone waited, watching the sea for the imminent invasion. Captain McMillin was certain it would come under the cover of darkness. He was correct.

At 2:15 the morning of Wednesday, December 10, 370 Japanese troops of 5th Company, Maizuri 2nd Special Naval Landing Force, came ashore at Dungcas Beach, about a mile northeast of Agaña. This group had spent the last few months on Saipan preparing specifically for an assault on Guam. They were familiar with every road and structure between the sea and the Government House. They quickly moved into Agaña proper, taking on the Insular Force Guard first and then the ten-man Marine guard at the governor's headquarters.

At the same time other Japanese forces, elements of the South Seas Detachment (SSD), landed at Tumon Bay, only a couple of miles north of Dungcas Beach. They encountered no resistance at all and quickly moved southwest along the coast, primarily using existing roadways. Two other groups landed at points southwest of Sumay and moved northeast to take on the Marines there, approaching from behind their positions. Another force came ashore at Talofofo Bay on the less populated eastern side of the island and marched northward toward the town of Yona and Yigo Bay, near the narrowest part of the landmass.

Most of these troops were seasoned and well-prepared, especially those with the battle-tested SSD force, made up of the 144th Infantry Regiment and some units that were part of the 55th Division. In all, the SSD had a strength of almost 5,000 men committed to the invasion of Guam.

Despite the months of planning and the considerable intelligence available to them, the Japanese invasion of Guam was not perfect. More troops of the SSD landed near Merizo at the far southwestern point of Guam. Those planning the invasion had decided correctly that the most resistance would certainly come from U.S. Marines on the Orote Peninsula. The orders to the SSD troops were to quickly march to Agat, just south of Sumay on the peninsula and where most of the Navy and Marine facilities were located, and approach from the east, leaving the Marines with no way to escape except into the water.

The invaders' intelligence had failed them on one detail, though, despite all the overflights during the past few months. There was no road up the coast from Merizo to the Orote Peninsula. The terrain was rough, almost impassable, and Mount Lamlam was in the way. The troops simply got back onto their ships, steamed northeastward up the coast, and went ashore again, this time just south of Agat, where they would still encounter little to no resistance as they met up with units who had already gone ashore nearby. From there, they had a good road to traverse to the peninsula, Sumay, and most of the anticipated U.S. Marine defenses.

For security purposes, none of the Japanese troops had been told their destination until after they left their staging areas on December 5. Except for the Merizo miscalculation, they were well prepared for the landing conditions they encountered, the reefs offshore, the narrow beaches, and the daunting cliffs that formed much of the island's shoreline.

Back on December 5, Guam time, Captain McMillin had received a terse, vague warning from his U.S. Navy commanders informing him that war could well be imminent and to prepare for possible armed conflict with the Japanese. One can only imagine his reaction. As if there really had been anything more he could have done to prepare.

For most of the Japanese troops, Haha Jima, in the Ogasawara group, south of the Home Islands, had been the location from which they had originally departed after having seen plenty of action in Manchuria. In all, about 5,900 battle-tested troops—sailors, marines, and infantry—made up the invasion force. They were supported by four heavy cruisers, two gunboats, six submarine chasers, two minesweepers, and two tenders. They also benefited from the two days of air assaults against Guam by an unknown number of aircraft from Rota and Tinian.

Defending the island were about 550 U.S. Marines and sailors.

It would later be determined that the Japanese had another flaw in their otherwise well-conceived plan. They had relied on yet another bit of inaccurate intelligence in planning the assault on Guam. Intelligence that led them to expect far more manpower and stiffer resistance than they would actually encounter. The Japanese force that conducted the First Battle of Guam was much larger than was necessary to accomplish their goal.

The primary battle of the very short invasion took place at the Plaza de España. That was adjacent to the Dulce Nombre de Maria Cathedral-Basilica, where Carmen Artero, her sister, Father Dueñas, and all the islanders had been taking part in the joyous Feast of the Immaculate Conception only two days before. But the initial objective of the invaders was the Government House and the governor himself, defended by ten Marines and a few members of the Insular Force Guard. The Japanese knew if they captured the Government House and took McMillin into custody, the American Marines might still offer pushback, but the island would quickly fall.

PFC Ray Church, the member of the unit assigned to protect the governor, remembers the perimeter of sandbags he and his fellow troops set up outside the headquarters building, looking out over the peaceful palm-tree-lined plaza and within sight of the historic Catholic church. They nicknamed their defensive position "the Last Stand."

Pedro Cruz was one of the three platoon leaders for the Insular Force Guard that had joined the Marines at Government House. He and his men manned the machine guns alongside Church and the other Marines. Cruz later recalled his primary goal that morning would be a simple one: "The only thought in my mind was, if I must die, I hope to God I kill some Japanese."

After shooting back and forth for most of an hour, there was a ceasefire at 5:45 a.m. Private Church later described the scene as the captain's adjutant emerged from the building behind them and ran down the front steps past them. He carried a broom handle with a white bedsheet tied to it. Waving the makeshift flag, he trotted toward where the Japanese troops had set up positions and were blasting away. Church held his breath, certain the aide would be gunned down. But the Japanese honored the white flag. The shooting promptly stopped.

Captain McMillin's formal letter of surrender was short and to the point:

Government House, Guam
10 December 1941

From: Governor of Guam
To: Senior Officer Present, Commanding Imperial Japanese Forces in Guam.
Subject: Surrender

1. I, Captain George J. McMillin, United States Naval Station, Guam, by authority of my commission from the President of the United States, do, as a result of superior military forces landed on Guam this date, as an act of war, surrender this post to you as the representative of the Imperial Japanese Government.

2. The responsibility of the civil government of Guam becomes yours as of the time of signing this document.

3. I have been assured by you that the civil rights of the population of Guam will be respected and that the military forces surrendered to you will be accorded all the rights stipulated by International Law and the laws of humanity.

(S) G. J. McMillin

Captain McMillin formally surrendered at 6:00 a.m., making Guam the first U.S. territory to be captured by Japan in World War II. Wake Island and two islands in the Aleutian chain of Alaska would be the only other American territories anywhere in the world occupied by troops of any enemy during the war. The United States would recapture the Aleutians a year later. Wake would remain in Japanese hands until after the end of the war.

As soon as McMillin informed the invaders that he was surrendering, word also went out to other U.S. military and civilian forces deployed around the island, including the larger contingent of Marines dug in on Orote Peninsula. They were told that the battle was over. All shooting was to stop. They were to lay down their arms and peacefully give themselves up to the invaders. Skirmishes continued around the island for the next few hours, but word finally reached everyone that the battle for Guam was over.

After the war, no blame was placed on anyone involved with the surrender. It would have been suicide to have continued to attempt to repel such a superior force. Captain George McMillin had no real choice, no matter how willingly and bravely his men would have continued the fight. Besides, with the declaration of a "category F" defensive status, the fate of the island had already been sealed should Japan decide they wanted it.

Church was proud that he and his small contingent were able to hold off the invaders for about forty-five minutes. The truth was, though, that they were already out of ammunition when the captain's aide dashed by them waving the white flag. Church was still lying behind the sandbags, partially beneath a bush, when the Imperial Japanese Army troops moved in. One of them flipped off the young Marine's helmet with a bayonet. Church was sure he would be executed then and there, but he was taken prisoner instead. He did witness one of the other Marine guards being bayoneted to death a few minutes later. Church never knew for sure why the Japanese had chosen to execute his friend. It was rumored that the unfortunate young Marine had a nervous tic with his eye. The invaders may have thought he was trying to signal someone.

The surrender event was awkward but quick. Captain McMillin, his second-in-command, and a contingent of the invaders stepped inside the Government House. The Japanese guard remained outside, tense, armed with rifles and fixed bayonets. The head of the primary Japanese invasion force, Major General Tomitaro Horii, an Imperial Japanese Army officer and commander of the South Seas Detachment, could speak no English. No one on the American side spoke Japanese. McMillin sent for several of the people of Japanese descent he had imprisoned earlier. They would need to interpret. It was a quick trip. They were in the jail across the plaza, only a short walk away.

There was little conversation. McMillin told the Japanese commander he was ready to sign the short letter of surrender. He did so and was ordered to stay there in the Government House with his aide and yeoman. They would remain there until that evening—"without food," McMillin would complain years later in his official report of the surrender—before the invasion troops moved him, his staff, and the rest of the Marine guards to the naval hospital.

In all, five U.S. Marines were killed and seventeen were wounded during the Japanese invasion of Guam. The Navy lost eight men killed in action, with eighteen wounded. Four Guam Insular Force Guards died in action, as did thirteen men, women, and children who were fleeing Agaña in a bus. That happened during the early stages of the invasion when Japanese troops opened fire on the vehicle. Then those in the bus who had not been killed outright were bayoneted by the Japanese. About thirty Guamanian civilians and one American civilian had died during the two days of air strikes. There would be many more deaths among civilians over the coming hours, days, and years.

Six sailors, including radioman George Tweed, decided not to stick around. Tweed had been sleeping soundly, worn out from trying to keep communications circuits online during the air strikes, when he heard the first rifle and machine-gun fire. He rolled over in his sack and saw it was about 3:00 a.m., far too early for the Leathernecks to be practicing. Then the sounds of field guns—weapons the Americans on the island were not fortunate enough to have—confirmed that the invasion they all had been anticipating was now underway. There had been much discussion among Tweed and his fellow sailors about what they would do if the Japanese did come to take the island.

First, of course, they would remain on duty at their assigned positions, ready to fight. But if surrender was a certainty, they could lay down their arms and give up, becoming POWs with an unknown fate. Or they could flee into the mountainous jungle and take their chances of surviving until America decided to charge back in and retake the island. That, they believed, would not be very long.

Tweed told his buddies he would never have a Japanese marine poking him in the backside with a bayonet. Besides, he had hiked all over Guam by then and thought he knew plenty of places he could hide for a month or two until the Navy came back. When he confirmed that the U.S. Marine guard had destroyed or disabled all the communications equipment at the Government House, and that Captain McMillin had given explicit permission for anyone under his command to disappear into the jungle should he choose to do so, Tweed and fellow radioman Al Tyson knew what they needed to do. They tried to make a run for it from the house where they were sleeping near the Plaza de España. They filled a satchel and a pillowcase with groceries, a blanket, and a flashlight, jumped into Tweed's car, then braved a barrage of machine-gun fire as they raced away. On the east side of the island, near the town of Yona, they abandoned the bullet-riddled vehicle, covered it over with brush, and disappeared into the thick jungle.

Four other sailors had come to the same decision. They, too, slipped away as the Japanese moved in. Chief Motor Machinist's Mate Michael Krump, Chief Aerographer L. W. Jones, Yeoman First Class Adolphe Yablonsky, and Machinist's Mate First Class C. B. Johnston fled into the rain forest to avoid capture.

Other than giving the Japanese control of the last of the Marianas and a strategic patch of ground in the Pacific, the spoils of the invasion of Guam were minimal. The yard patrol boat *YP-17* was damaged, but the Japanese repaired the vessel and made use of it. The oil depot ship *Robert L. Barnes* was also salvaged and put to some use, since nearby fuel storage tanks had been destroyed in the air assaults. Ammunition at the Marine magazine and 5,000 gallons of oil were burned before the surrender, but 4,000 gallons of aviation fuel in a Pan Am storage tank was claimed by the invaders. All military communications equipment had been destroyed when it was obvious the Japanese were coming. While most heavy trucks belonging to the military had been made inoperable, functioning automobiles and trucks on the island—military or civilian—became the property of the Japanese.

After the surrender and formally taking control of Guam, one of the first orders of business for Major General Tomitaro Horii was to rename the island. It would now be known as Omiya Jima, or "Great Shrine Island." The name of the town of Agaña was changed to Akashi ("Bright Red Stone"). Other towns on the island were given new Japanese names as well.

In announcing the successful "liberation" of Guam, by order of the supreme emperor, the Japanese commander in chief stated the rationale for the action.

"It is for the purpose of restoring liberty and rescuing the whole Asiatic people and creating the permanent peace in Asia. Thus, our intention is to establish the New Order of the World."

There was further assurance to the civilian population of Guam that things were about to get markedly better for each of them now that the Empire of Japan had come to their rescue. A notice in English went out to everyone, promising, "You good citizens need not worry anything [sic] under the regulations of our Japanese authorities and my [sic] enjoy your daily life as we guarantee your lives and never distress nor plunder your property."

Major General Horii had earlier in the war expressed dismay at the brutal atrocities committed by some Japanese troops once they took control of new territory and its civilian population. He even wrote and distributed a pamphlet, titled *Guide to Soldiers in the South Seas*, in which he ordered that troops under his command would not needlessly kill or injure local inhabitants, that looting and violating women would be strictly forbidden, that buildings and property would not be burned—without permission from senior officers—and that they would "treat ammunition carefully, reducing waste to a minimum." The members of the SSD force had each received a copy of the pamphlet prior to the invasion of Guam.

American military prisoners, including Captain McMillin and Lieutenant Colonel William MacNulty, the commander of the Marines on Guam, were kept on the island for several weeks before being put on a ship bound for Formosa. Most of them were eventually moved to Manchuria, while some went to

Japan. Regardless of where they ended up, they experienced unbelievably horrible treatment and performed forced labor as POWs for the rest of the war. And many did not survive the ordeal.

One of those POWs was Captain George McMillin. The governor's captors took him to the Japanese Home Island of Shikoku. He and his fellow prisoners were among the very first American POWs of the war, and regardless of where he was being held, Captain McMillin was usually the oldest captive there. He had just turned fifty-two years old at the time of the invasion of Guam. The few American civilians who were still on Guam at the time of the invasion, along with the four Navy nurses, were held as prisoners there on the island until they eventually became part of a diplomatic exchange, completed in June 1942. From there, they went home to the United States.

Another prisoner of war was the young sailor Edward Howard, the crew member of the old minesweeper *Penguin*. He was the one who looked back as they escaped the scuttled vessel and watched the American flag disappear beneath the waters of Apra Harbor. Howard grew up on a farm in Indiana and planned to attend DePauw University. But, like many, he had a desire for adventure before settling down and maybe becoming a farmer, so he enlisted in the Navy in 1938 at the age of eighteen. He was soon assigned to the *Penguin* and was stationed on the island of Guam.

There Howard met, fell in love with, and married a beautiful Chamorro girl named Maria Aguon Perez but known as Mariquita. They soon had two children, a boy and a girl, both born on Guam. The girl was a newborn when the Japanese attack came. That made his capture and eventual removal from the island even more traumatic than it was for the other sailors.

Howard would later remember much yelling and shoving by their captors as he and his fellow Americans laid down their arms and surrendered. Suddenly a Japanese soldier ripped Howard's shirt off him, pulled out a sword, and ordered him to kneel. The sailor was certain he was about to be beheaded. But after posturing for a bit, placing the sharp edge of the sword against the sailor's neck, the soldier finally laughed and motioned for him to stand up and march along behind the other prisoners. The Japanese had good use for strong young captives.

Howard would not see his wife or children before he and the others were shipped off the island, nor would he know how they and his in-laws had fared. But before he was gone, Mariquita was able to give him something that would provide him and his fellow POWs great comfort over the coming long, hard years. Edward and Mariquita had begun attending a Protestant church on Guam even though she was a lifelong Catholic. He would later remember, "At home, we would read the Bible and pray together. It was a wonderful time."

Mariquita was somehow able, at great risk, to slip a Bible to her husband before he was taken off Guam and sent far away from her and their babies. It would later help him endure unbelievably bad times and eventual heartbreak.

It would not be long before the gentle, fun-loving, friendly people of "Great Shrine Island" realized that "liberty" and being "rescued" by the Japanese was not a good thing for them at all. That was despite the promises made and the instructions included in Major General Horii's pamphlet. Even so, most were certain—or at least hopeful—that the United States would come back soon and save them from the brutality that was almost immediately inflicted on them by the occupiers. That involved forced labor by men, women, and children, harsh restrictions on daily life, sexual assaults, rationing of food and other necessities, lack of medicine and medical services, and vicious retribution—including beheadings or other public executions—for those who broke the strict and often arbitrary rules of the occupation. Punishment was especially severe, even deadly, for anyone suspected of harboring military men who were rumored to have escaped into the hills and jungle during the assault.

As it happened, that hoped-for return by the Americans would not be so soon in coming. Many Chamorros predicted the war would not last one hundred days. The mighty United States of America would now rise up and put an end to this nonsense. But the islanders would not learn until after the war that the actual Japanese plan all along was not only to occupy Guam for at least one hundred years but to strive to make it a part of the Empire for at least a thousand. Nor would they know until later that the liberation of Guam was hardly a given.

The decision on whether or not to take Guam back would ultimately depend on a fateful choice between two very different plans, one proposed by General Douglas MacArthur, the other by Admiral Chester Nimitz.

In truth, the long, dreadful ordeal for the people of Guam had just begun. And they would see that Captain McMillin's hopes in his formal surrender document, the assumptions about the civil rights of the islanders, and adherence to international law and "the laws of humanity" were not to be.

★ CHAPTER THREE ★

CREATING THE PERMANENT PEACE

Another of the first tasks for the Japanese after completing the brief takeover of Guam was to order the Chamorros to get to work burying the bodies of their friends and neighbors who had died in the invasion. Antonio Palomo, only ten years old at the time, later remembered his father telling him that he had personally buried thirty of his neighbors who died in the assault. That was hard news to comprehend for a such a young boy.

Many of the islanders, like Antonio and the family of young Carmen Artero, had fled from the areas around Agaña and Sumay to their ranches, which were spread out around Guam, in an effort to get as far away from the invaders as they could. Many had no choice: as many as 2,000 people in Sumay alone were evicted from their homes to provide shelter for the invaders. The people simply had to find places elsewhere to live.

Japanese troops went from village to village, from ranch to ranch, and left leaflets assuring residents that their lives would soon be remarkably better as part of the Empire of Japan than it had ever been as an overlooked and exploited possession of the United States. The claim was that the Japanese, fellow Asians, had liberated the Chamorros from American colonialism. From this point on, they promised to do all they could to erase any signs of the forty-three-year "occupation" by the Americans and, before that, the Spanish.

However, those same leaflets ordered citizens to surrender all weapons they had in their possession. It would now be illegal for any Guam civilian to have a gun. They also were to turn over any communications equipment, including broadcast and shortwave receivers, whether they were functioning or not. All American currency was to be swapped promptly for Japanese yen at a grossly unfair one-to-one exchange rate. Dollars were no longer to be accepted by any merchant. Effective immediately, only the Japanese language was to be taught in schools, and those few who returned to school after the takeover also had to learn and sing patriotic Japanese songs. Merchants were required to change the signage on their businesses, replacing English with Japanese. Rationing of food and medicine started at once, too, and anyone guilty of hoarding or refusing to share with troops would be made an example.

Every citizen was required to carry a pass issued by the new government. It consisted of a piece of cloth with Japanese characters. No one would be allowed to move about on the island without the pass. Anyone doing so was subject to serious punishment.

Every man, woman, and child on the island was to register at once with the occupation forces. Islanders soon learned one reason for that requirement: anyone able to do manual labor would be required to do so. "Able" was a very loose description. Even children, women, the infirm, and the elderly would have to help build roads, barracks, military fortifications, and more, or work in the rice paddies and fields. Or help clear jungle to plant more. Troops seemed to be arriving every day, and they needed locally grown food to eat.

The first major construction project would be to expand the runway at the airfield at Sumay on the Orote Peninsula. Land would also be cleared for another airstrip a couple of miles east of Agaña, with work beginning on at least three more landing strips at various spots around the island. It seemed the Japanese intended to land airplanes on every parcel of relatively flat ground on the island. Clearly, the Japanese intended to put Guam to use as a major air facility and a staging area for troops bound for other islands in the Marianas, the Philippines, and across the South Pacific.

A typical job for men, women, and children was to carry large bags of gravel to the new runway site, dump it, and go back several miles for more, on foot, in the heat of the tropical sun. They used a long pole with a big basket tied in the middle. The basket was filled with the gravel and the workers placed the pole on their shoulders to carry the backbreaking load.

Most would not know what kind of work they were going to be doing until they showed up each morning about sunrise for a roll call. Then they would receive their assignments for the day. Workdays were typically ten to twelve hours long, with inadequate food and water and precious little time to rest. Anyone considered to be a slacker was subject to a beating.

Islander Antonio Calvo remembered his first job was to go visit farmers across the island and collect milk, eggs, meat, fruits, and vegetables and bring it all back for the troops. Anyone not turning over all the produce they had on hand was supposed to be reported by Calvo to the soldiers in charge. Then the islanders holding back food would receive brutal punishment. Even so, farmers soon found ways to hide pigs and chickens so the invaders would not take all they had. That was the only way they were able to continue to feed their families. Carmen Artero, Antonio Paloma, and others would later describe the creative ways their families found to prepare naturally grown fruits, vegetables, and roots, just to have something to eat.

Within days, though, Antonio Calvo started a new job. He and other men were ordered to use axes to cut down the tallest coconut trees they could find. Then they sawed the trunks into sections ten feet long. Next, they were given brushes and buckets of black paint. They were to paint the trees and then carry them one at a time by hand more than four miles to the cliffs overlooking the sea. There they dug holes in the cliff face and installed the tree trunks to look like cannons, aimed out over the sea, toward any potential approaching invaders. Actual cannons and antiaircraft guns were arrayed farther back from the bluffs. The purpose of the ruse was for any attackers by air to

waste their bombs on the dummy cannons and then be susceptible to fire from the real ones.

Another Guam native, Juan Pangelinan, would later vividly
describe how inhumanely their occupiers treated everyone.
They would be slapped in the face or walloped on the back with
a cane or bullwhip—or, at times, a sword—for absolutely no reason. If an islander approached a Japanese soldier, he or she was
required to stop and bow. Anytime anyone walked past a building used by the military—whether there was anyone inside or
even in sight—Chamorros were supposed to stop, stand at attention, then bow. Soldiers also would stop people at random
and force them to bow toward the north, in the direction of the
Empire and Emperor Hirohito, as a show of respect and loyalty.
Not doing so resulted in punishment.

Pangelinan's girlfriend—and future wife—was half Japanese,
which made her of special interest to the occupiers. When they
learned from her that she had a fiancé and who he was, they
called Pangelinan in and threatened to punish him if he did not
leave the young woman alone. He refused. But when the Japanese soldier pulled out his sword and slammed it hard onto the
desk in front of him, Pangelinan reluctantly agreed to stop seeing her.

But then, when his girlfriend boldly stood her ground, she
was beaten. She eventually relented. Juan and his fiancé did not
stop seeing each other, of course. But from that point on, they
were very careful about it.

Mariquita Howard was not so fortunate. The wife of Edward, the Indiana sailor from the *Penguin* who was now a POW,

the mother of his girl and boy, was a beautiful woman. She unintentionally attracted the attention of a high-ranking Japanese officer. He ordered her to have sex with him. She refused. The officer had Mariquita executed.

Mariquita's parents would care for the two children for the rest of the war. And Edward Howard would not know the fate of his wife and kids for another four years.

Such behavior became marginally less common after the Japanese military used five of the confiscated houses to bring in "comfort girls" from Tokyo for the soldiers. Even so, Carmen Artero would remember witnessing troops openly assaulting women, fondling them, making crude gestures, and obscenely mocking them. She would hear of rapes and other mistreatment of girls and women. Carmen's mother always hid her and her sister whenever Japanese soldiers approached their ranch. She also recalled times when a platoon of soldiers would suddenly barge into their house, ransack the place, find all the food they could, then sit down at their table and eat it all as the family looked on, knowing they would have to go hungry.

By order of the Japanese commander, ownership of any private businesses was turned over to the occupation forces. The South Seas Development Company, a Japanese enterprise owned by the government, assumed control of all businesses on the island as well as all commerce to and from Guam. Now all the Marianas had been brought under the auspices of the Greater East Asia Co-Prosperity Sphere, a concept the Empire of Japan claimed would bring together all peoples of Asian descent. It actually meant any natural resources and foodstuff not needed to keep the islanders alive went onto ships bound for Japan.

The Japanese also often used the phrase "Asia for the Asians" in an attempt to convince the countries they were bringing into their Empire, one way or another, that they would be Asians looking out for and defending other Asians against the white American and European colonialists who had gobbled up and ruled much of the region throughout history. The Japanese, fellow Asians, were displacing European masters such as the Spanish, Dutch, British, and French, as well as the Americans. The primary reason for Japanese expansion, though, was simply because a modern industrial nation required iron ore, coal, rubber, petroleum, chrome, tin, and other natural resources unavailable on the Home Islands. And with a population of more than 73 million in 1940, with most of the people involved in supporting the expansion of the Empire, they needed food, too. The Japanese resented being held hostage and having the Empire's growth stunted because of the lack of such materials.

Manchuria was a primary early target for Japanese takeover, because the area was rich in iron and coal as well as plenty of hardy people who could be forced to mine it. It was also a source for wheat, soybeans, meat, and other food as well as another primary need: cotton. Plus, Manchuria was practically next door.

Japan's military strength was often underestimated by the countries that came into their sights. That typically led to quick invasions by well-trained and motivated troops. By June of 1942, the Empire of Japan reached from Manchuria in the north to New Guinea in the south. From east to west, Japanese control extended to Assam, on the eastern border of India, and to the Gilbert Islands, southeast of Hawaii, in the South Pacific Ocean. There were already plans being discussed for the invasion of

Australia, but continued heavy fighting and troop commitments against China required putting those on the back burner. Having the United States now in the fray and quickly cranking up its war machine nixed the Australian plans, too. Now, with the capture of the final piece of the Mariana puzzle, Japan concentrated on Malaya, the Philippines, and the Dutch East Indies, as well as shoring up defenses in all territories captured so far. As long as they could control the shipping lanes from the captured territories to the Japanese Home Islands, they were confident they could regroup and then continue expansion. Maybe all the way to India and then the oil fields of the Middle East, where they would find petroleum to power the Empire as well as its allies, Germany and Italy.

In truth, Guam offered nothing in the way of the natural resources and agricultural products so desperately sought by Japan. Its importance to the Greater East Asia Co-Prosperity Sphere was its location on the Philippine Sea and the central Pacific Ocean. Even so, the invaders took advantage of every opportunity to bring local merchants into the South Seas Development Company as quickly as they could. And any place on which they did not plan to build an airstrip or housing for troops, they began growing rice and digging in weapon emplacements, bunkers, and tunnels.

Once their mission was completed, the South Seas Detachment and their commander, Major General Tomitaro Horii, left Guam in mid-January 1942, bound for another larger island where there were even bigger ambitions. They had captured Guam with minimal loss of strength and, through intimidation and brutality, had quickly brought the island's residents under the complete control of the occupiers. Now, with the unit's reputation for ruthlessness firmly intact, the SSD was bound for Rabaul, New Britain, in New Guinea, where they would assist in a quick, deadly invasion and brutal takeover from primarily Australian troops. Despite that area's recent history of volcanic activity, the Japanese would soon build it up as one of their most powerful bases. At one point in 1943, more than 110,000 troops would be billeted there.

The departure of the South Seas Detachment gave the Chamorros and others on Guam some hope that the harsh treatment might ease up a bit. Once in New Britain, the SSD force would be involved in one of the most horrific atrocities of the war, the outright murder of 160 Australian prisoners of war. Many of the POWs were chased into the jungle only to be bayoneted by SSD troops, in hiding and awaiting them. Other prisoners were lined up and shot point-blank.

But back on Guam, the hope by the Chamorros was that things would get better with the SSD and Major General Horii gone and inflicting their hellish treatment on somebody else. However, any improvement was insignificant.

For the duration of their occupation of Guam, the enemy force continued their efforts to convince the Chamorro people of Japanese superiority over the Americans and that the war would soon result in victory for the Empire, of which they were now and forevermore a part. Each time there was a Japanese victory somewhere, there would be a big military parade through the streets of Agaña. Ultimately, most of the processions, featuring platoons of soldiers threateningly brandishing their swords, ended at a Buddhist shrine on a hill overlooking

Agaña. Residents were required to turn out and enthusiastically cheer for each success.

When Singapore fell in February 1942, there were parades through the streets of not only the primary towns but also the smaller villages, including San Nicolas and San Ignacio, an indication of how important the Japanese believed that victory to be. There were other, especially fervent demonstrations when word came that General Douglas MacArthur and his family had been chased from the Philippines to Australia, and then again in May when the Philippines fell to Japanese forces.

These victory parades typically featured a vehicle decorated as a float that portrayed a youngster wearing the uniform of a Japanese soldier. Throughout the route, the young boy was compelled to stand with one foot on the American flag as he pointed a rifle at another young boy who wore a U.S. Navy uniform.

George Tweed, the Navy radioman, and the other five sailors who had escaped into the jungle during the Japanese invasion, had found shelter and received food, clothing, and other supplies from the Chamorros. The Guamanians were willing to help despite the danger and constant threats by the occupiers of what would happen to them if anyone did.

Tweed and Al Tyson, the other sailor who had braved the machine-gun fire to speed away, decided to split up, reasoning it would be easier to avoid capture that way. Tweed primarily stuck to territory he had hiked over during his long stay on the island. He was constantly on the lookout for secluded ravines or caves deep enough in the jungle to avoid accidentally encountering a Japanese patrol but close enough so Chamorros could bring him food and other supplies. He tried to move often, knowing one slip of the tongue or one person fearing for the safety of himself or his family might divulge where he was. Tweed assumed getting caught would result in a quick and ugly execution.

While he was hiding, he managed to fix a broken Silvertone brand radio receiver, one that had been confiscated by the troops from a former Navy building. Some of the natives had boldly swiped it from a Japanese storehouse in the hopes they would be able to hear some news about how the war was going. Tweed recognized the radio set. He had worked on this very one before and had planned to once again get it working when he had a chance. The invasion had prevented that.

Now he knew exactly what it would take to fix it. He just did not know where he was going to get the parts he needed to do it. Against all odds and at great risk, someone was able to locate, steal, and bring to him the very components he needed. Someone else secured an electrical generator to power the radio. That allowed him to monitor news broadcasts, including a regular nightly roundup from shortwave station KGEI, located in San Francisco, California. The outlet was owned by General Electric with studios in the Fairmont Hotel. It had a powerful transmitter and antenna array located near what is now Redwood City. At the time, the station was the only source of reliable news for most of the South Pacific and Asia—especially the areas occupied by Japanese troops—with newscasts and programs specifically beamed to that part of the world each night.

George Tweed was not the only one making use of the resurrected radio. Often, as many as a dozen people would huddle together in Tweed's cave, listening to the newscasts as they faded in and out. That was their only way of keeping up with what was happening in the world beyond the shores of their own island. Soon, using a typewriter and carbon paper someone brought him, Tweed began "publishing" the *Guam Eagle*, a printed summary of the stories gleaned from the broadcasts he heard on KGEI. The newspaper was limited to only five copies because of the carbon paper's capabilities. Despite that, it received wide circulation. People would take them from house to house and read them aloud to everyone who wanted to hear the latest. Then each copy was burned so it would not fall into Japanese hands and possibly lead them to Tweed. Those who distributed the crude news source were risking their lives in doing so.

Like the islanders, the six sailors who had escaped into the jungle on the morning of the invasion assumed that the Japanese occupation would be short-lived—that the United States would soon reclaim Guam and rescue them. The men were betting their lives that they could stay hidden and healthy until then, and not end up in a POW camp somewhere. Or worse. Word was that the Japanese were especially miffed by anyone who had dared to escape and who might still be hiding on the island. They considered them to be a threat to their authority and put emphasis on their capture.

As the occupiers settled in, pressure increased on the Chamorros to turn in any American servicemen that might still be evading capture. The Japanese knew the sailors could not possibly remain hidden on such a small chunk of land without considerable help from the people of the island. There was plenty of confirmation that as many as half a dozen U.S. Navy men remained at large on the island in defiance of the new regime. They even knew the identity of at least one of them. The occupation force offered a bounty of 100 yen for anyone who turned in a fugitive American sailor. But the reward was 1,000 yen for the radioman, George Ray Tweed.

That increased price on Tweed's head was because of his value as a radioman and the possibility that he would somehow find a way to communicate with other U.S. military units out there somewhere. Some Chamorros whom the Japanese suspected knew the general whereabouts of the escapees were arrested and harassed. They refused to reveal any information of value. They were tortured, jailed, and beaten. Others were publicly decapitated merely for being suspected of harboring the Americans or just knowing their general whereabouts. The executions were also intended to convince those who did have knowledge to step forward and tell what they knew.

Although they were aware that it was wise to remain dispersed, the six escapees did meet up several times over the ten months they all remained at large. In some hole in the ground somewhere, they sat around a small fire, drank *tuba*—an alcoholic beverage made from the sap of the coconut palm tree—and told tales of constructing their hideouts, of ideas that had worked and those that had not, of means to avoid illness and treat various injuries, and of their considerable close calls with enemy soldiers. Talk inevitably turned to family back home and the reality that everyone probably assumed the worst fate had befallen their sons, husbands, brothers, and fathers on Guam. Mostly, though, they laughed about and made light of their appearance, their sailor uniforms now ragged and dirty, their uncut and filthy hair and beards. The two chief petty officers in the group, Krump and Jones, still insisted on trying to wear their CPO hats, but it had become difficult to keep them on their heads because their hair was so long and matted. Despite the danger, the men saw their few brief reunions in firelit caves as therapeutic, maybe even worth the risk, as the months passed with no hint of any impending U.S. invasion. It certainly relieved some of the constant tension when they could relax with their fellow runaway "shipmates."

The relentless, brutal pressure being applied to the people of Guam in relation to the escaped sailors finally paid off for the Japanese. On September 12, 1942, they captured sailors Michael Krump, L. W. Jones, and Adolphe Yablonsky after their jungle hiding spot was revealed to them by a Guam native. The Chamorro had turned the men in for the bounty, yes, but even more because he feared for his own life and that of his family. Once the Japanese knew that he had knowledge of the sailors' hideout, he felt he had no choice. And the Japanese also promised the man that the fugitives would not be harmed. That they would just be sent away to become well-treated prisoners of war for the duration of the conflict. Life would be better for them than cowering in the wilds of Guam.

The sailors had already agreed among themselves not to resist if they faced arrest. They had no weapons or other way of defending themselves. So, when the time came, they simply gave themselves up peacefully, trusting they would become POWs like their comrades who surrendered on the day of the invasion. And as the Japanese had signaled to them from day one. There was no trial or incarceration for the captured men. They were promptly lined up, told to kneel, and beheaded by sword-wielding soldiers. Their bodies were photographed, and those pictures would be circulated widely so the other fugitives and those harboring them might see them. And then the three men were buried in a single grave, in the soil they had once vowed to defend.

Just over a month later, Tweed's fellow radioman, Al Tyson—the Japanese were apparently unaware of his job, as he had so far not commanded the higher bounty—and C. B. Johnston were located and surrounded by fifty Japanese troops after a tip from two more Chamorros. The men gave themselves up without a fight. And once more, the two sailors were executed, this time by gunfire, and buried on the spot.

That left only Howard Ray Tweed, the radioman from Oregon.

It is miraculous that Tweed somehow remained on the loose. There were rumblings that one reason the Japanese occupiers were so cruel in their treatment of the people of Guam was because some of them insisted on stubbornly sheltering the American, moving him around to eleven different locations during the more than two years of Japanese control. Several Guam natives died at the hands of the occupiers as a direct result of his presence. Some of those who lost their lives had helped Tweed along the way. Others had not, but they were suspected of having done so. There was even resentment among some Chamorros that Tweed regularly received food while many of their families went hungry. And there were plenty of rumors that he was having relationships with some young Chamorro women. But many still believed that as long as one American remained alive on the island, it would make it more likely that the Navy and Marines would return and put an end to their nightmare. Tweed continued to provide them with news from the outside world as well, preventing total isolation.

Life was hardly easy for the U.S. Marines and sailors who had surrendered and become prisoners of war during the enemy invasion rather than slip away and hide in the jungle and mountains. After their capture, Private Ray Church and his fellow Government House guards were held in an old church building. They were given no food or water and had to scrounge for anything they could find to eat.

Days turned into weeks. Then, without notice, the Marines were marched all the way to the navy yard near Piti. It was a tough trek, as they were so weak from hunger. At the navy yard they were divided into groups of five, loaded onto the ships, and marched all the way to the lowest deck. Seven days later they were in Japan, being taken off the ships in the glow of glaring spotlights, which were there to make sure nobody could escape into the darkness. There were also the flashbulbs of reporters, supposedly there to show the world how humanely Japan was treating its prisoners of war.

Even though it was winter, the captives were quickly processed and put to work. For their first task, they were forced to clear brush and rocks from a plot of land in order that sweet potatoes could be planted there.

Church, the Mormon Marine from small-town Utah, and his fellow prisoners had no idea of the length and depth of the ordeal that had just begun. An ordeal that would last almost three and a half years and one that many of them would not survive.

Meanwhile, after the capture and deaths of the two fugitive

sailors in October, George Tweed suspected that the net was being drawn tighter and his capture might be looming. He determined it would be prudent to move to the large ranch owned by the family of Antonio Artero, located in the far north part of Guam. Artero agreed. There Tweed became even more careful about his own movements and about allowing more than a few people to know his whereabouts. Even those he trusted. He understood the deadly pressure to betray him that the Japanese continued to put on the islanders.

It was there, at the remote ranch, that Tweed would hide out for the better part of two years, constantly in fear of discovery. Eventually, though, he would play a small role in the Second Battle of Guam. And a bold promise Tweed made to Antonio Artero, the Agaña meat shop and ranch owner, would one day be fulfilled.

On the Japanese side, army sergeant Shoichi Yokoi's experience was typical of many of his fellow invasion force troops. A citizen of the Aichi Prefecture, he had been an apprentice tailor when he was drafted into the army in 1941 and whisked away for training. But his loyalty to the emperor and his country was without question. Yokoi became a member of the 29th Infantry Division in Manchuria, where he quickly moved up to the rank of sergeant. In February 1943, at the age of twenty-eight, he was transferred to the 38th Regiment in the Mariana Islands and arrived on Guam. There he served in the unglamorous job of a supply sergeant.

It would be about a year and a half later that Shoichi's story would suddenly veer in a dramatically different direction from that of most of his fellow Japanese soldiers who were similarly billeted on the island. Amazingly, he would ultimately serve his country for an additional twenty-eight years, all of that time still on the island of Guam. He and his loyalty and dedication to the emperor of Japan would become yet another fascinating footnote to the story of the island during World War II and for almost three decades afterward. And Shoichi's experiences would make his name known around the world.

As the occupation dragged on through 1942, 1943, and the early months of 1944, the Chamorros began to notice signs—and got confirmation from the shortwave broadcasts and the *Guam Eagle*—that the war had taken a downturn for the Empire of Japan. Islands to the east of Guam were falling one after the other, like dominoes. Falling, but not easily. Still, the news was heartening.

There were also intensified efforts by the Japanese occupational forces to build up defenses on Guam. Then came a massive influx of Japanese troops pulled in from other battle zones. They were obviously elite troops, well equipped, ready to defend Guam, and, most likely, to be used to blunt any move by the Allies to reclaim the Philippines. Combat forces on the island eventually reached about 20,000 men, roughly equivalent to the Chamorro population of the island when the war started.

The occupiers had already put into place a plan to make the island self-supporting, which required a big emphasis on agriculture. The Japanese had decided that they would need enough food production on Guam to support as many as 30,000 troops for as long as it took to protect this flank of the Empire. A new, specialized group showed up not to fight but to increase the efficiency of agriculture there. They brought with them farm machinery, plows, cultivators, and more.

The new equipment did not make the burden on the Chamorros any easier. They were still utilized to do the heavy manual labor that was required to produce the desired crop yields and to prepare the island for the long-awaited invasion by the Allies. Many continued to work on the airstrips that were under construction in various spots. Others helped build pillboxes, barriers, and deep tunnels, digging out caves even deeper into the mountainsides. Others built and put into place large cemented-coral barricades along the beaches. Men continued cutting coconut trees and installing them as fake artillery along the coastal bluffs. Women were required to plant and harvest farm crops, especially rice.

Along the southern coast of the island, Chamorros cut more coconut trees and then arrayed the trunks across roadways as obstacles for American tanks and other vehicles. Despite the heat and humidity, still more forced laborers dug up rocks and carried them to the beaches, piling them in mounds, while others dug trenches and pits in the sand to make it more difficult for vehicles and troops to come ashore.

In a true act of desperation, a group of men was ordered to hunt down and kill every dog on Guam. The Japanese explained that, if there should be an invasion by the Americans, dogs might reveal the hiding places of Japanese soldiers lying in ambush.

While conditions became even worse for the natives of Guam, the limited news they heard and the seemingly frantic actions of their occupiers now offered renewed hope. Maybe the war would end soon for them. The Americans were finally coming back to set them free. Surely the powerful United States military would make quick work of the invasion, too, with minimal damage and bloodshed.

Unfortunately, the Chamorros had no way of knowing just how ghastly the days leading up to that long-anticipated invasion would be for them. And just how much death and destruction would soon follow.

Meanwhile, from his initial prison camp on the island of Formosa, Captain George McMillin had been, quite surprisingly, allowed to write several letters to his wife, Annabel, who now lived in California. He put on a happy face for her, but he was likely aware that the Japanese were monitoring, censoring, and maybe even enhancing his words, using them for propaganda purposes. According to a story in the *Vindicator*, his hometown newspaper in Youngstown, Ohio, McMillin wrote Annabel that his health was "splendid." Later, after a move to the prison camp on Shikoku, the former naval governor of Guam was interviewed by a reporter. The article ran in newspapers around the United States reporting that McMillin felt "chipper."

In truth, the captain had one primary goal for the interview. He told the reporter that he wanted to make certain that President Franklin D. Roosevelt was fully aware of one thing.

The island of Guam had been "valiantly defended."

★ CHAPTER FOUR ★

OPERATION FORAGER

A n island once deemed nonessential, a territory not to be vigorously defended, eventually became a key element in the plans of the United States and its Allies. Land that must be reclaimed. That change of emphasis took shape in late 1943. Such is the nature of strategic and then tactical decisions, with evolving needs dictated by the results of previously executed judgments. Sweeping choices directly impacting the lives of hundreds of thousands of men and women warriors and countless civilians. That and altering the course of history. And those determinations are often made only after great discord and discussion among powerful leaders charged with moving about all the pieces on the chessboard.

During 1943 and the first half of 1944, the Allies captured the Solomon Islands, the Gilbert Islands, the Marshall Islands, and the Papuan Peninsula of New Guinea. Many among the Allies now believed the war in the South Pacific had turned in their favor after a discouraging start. Others noted that there was still a long way to go. The Japanese were still very much in control of much of China and Manchuria, the Philippines, the Caroline Islands, the Palau Islands, and the Mariana Islands, as well as Taiwan. They had the benefit of years of preparation, too.

By late 1943, Admiral Chester Nimitz had already made key decisions on how to press the enemy. Among them was to bypass the Carolines and Palau Islands. Instead, they would zoom right past those outposts and aggressively launch major assaults on and claim the key islands in the Marianas, including Guam. They would also prepare to attack the Japanese-occupied island of Formosa. And, of course, take back the Philippines.

There were two primary reasons for the renewed interest in the Mariana chain, and neither had anything to do with rescuing the Chamorros or reclaiming captured American soil on Guam. The first reason was to have a base of operations from which to help take back the Philippines, just to the other side of the Philippine Sea. The Marianas also happened to be well placed to support the eventual invasion of the Japanese homeland. With the capture of the Marianas, the Allies would once again control important communications circuits, actual wires that snaked between the Home Islands and their captured territory to the south and southwest, including the Philippines.

The other factor, and by far the primary reason that changed minds about the value of the Marianas, was that the islands were perfectly situated to take advantage of recent developments in aircraft technology. They could provide the needed base of operations to support almost continual massive bombing of Japan by the recently perfected B-29 Superfortresses.

The plan was finally approved, put into place, and then formally launched in November 1943 under the code name "Operation Cartwheel." In addition to U.S. forces, the Allied effort included ships, troops, and aircraft from Australia, New Zealand, the Netherlands, and other islands around the Pacific.

Some of the specific details of the plans for Operation Cartwheel had been a major point of contention, however. Powerful leaders have powerful personalities. General Douglas MacArthur, commander of the Southwest Pacific Area, was adamant that the bulk of the forces head north through New Guinea, then quickly move on westward with the intent of fulfilling his famous and dramatic promise to return to the Philippines.

Some, primarily in the Navy, felt forces should instead island-hop through the central Pacific, then eventually arrive in the Marianas. From there, they could more easily aim the point of their spear northward, up the spine of islands that seemed to offer well-placed stepping-stones directly to Japan. Admiral Chester Nimitz, commander in chief, U.S. Pacific Fleet and Pacific Ocean Areas, was the primary advocate for that tack. He believed that after taking the Marianas, Allied forces could go on to capture Taiwan, Iwo Jima, Okinawa, and, eventually, proceed with the massive invasion of the Home Islands, a bold operation that was already well into the planning stages.

Additionally, Nimitz felt that from Taiwan the Allies would be able to control more effectively all oceangoing traffic from the Philippines and other Japanese-held territories in Southeast

Asia. That would make it easier to then take back the Philippines while continuing to choke off the supply of natural resources to Japan and its war machine.

Military historians would later declare that MacArthur, to a
certain extent, won that battle, but Nimitz got his way, too.
MacArthur, the man who would be called "the American Cae-
sar," generally won arguments such as this. At the highest level,
it was decided that U.S. forces would take both routes. So it was
determined that MacArthur would continue to amass a huge
force and cut a path by the most direct route to the Philippines,
the country from which he, his family, and his staff had been
unceremoniously chased in March of 1942.

Meanwhile, Admiral Nimitz and his forces would proceed
through the central Pacific, making their way to the Marianas
and beyond. Their goal was to attack and claim the Marianas by
mid-1944. Then, as soon as landing strips could be made ready
on Guam, Saipan, and Tinian, strategic incendiary bombing of
Japanese cities would commence. Bombing not just of military
targets but of whole cities, all in the hope that the Japanese
people would rise up and demand that the military and Emperor Hirohito call a halt to this deadly, brutal war before the
Home Islands were wiped off the map.

From Guam, Tinian, and Saipan, the Boeing B-29 Superfortress bombers, with a range of at least 3,200 miles, could reach
Japan much more easily. Even when carrying 10,000 pounds of
bombs, the Superfortresses could fly in, do their deadly, destructive work, and make it back to the Marianas with fuel to spare.
They were also capable of flying at an altitude of just over 31,000
feet, which put them out of reach of most of the Empire's fighter

aircraft and antiaircraft artillery. These new aircraft were designed for precisely the high-altitude strategic bombing that the United States was already conducting over the Home Islands, except they were doing it from more distant airfields in China. But they were also very adept at low-altitude missions to drop incendiary bombs, which was now a major part of the strategy, and also for dropping naval mines to help in the blockade of Japan. Basing the B-29s in the Marianas would also allow them to assist in the invasion of the Philippines, since they were only about 1,500 miles east of Manila.

That, then, was the primary reason Guam and her sister islands were back on the radar. And why plans were made for a major assault on the Japanese-held Mariana Islands in June 1944.

The operation was designated "Operation Forager." A forager is someone who goes from place to place looking for something he or she can use. The code name for the invasion of Guam would be "Stevedore." The attempt to reclaim the Philippines was "Operation Musketeer I, II, and III." And it all fed into the most daunting goal of all: "Operation Downfall," the eventual invasion of the Japanese homeland.

The latter was something dreaded by all but considered ultimately necessary to bring the war to an end. The only other way would be for the Japanese people, for the first time in their existence, to question the wisdom of their emperor and demand a surrender. Few believed they would do that. Most Japanese still believed in the "Sacred Wind," the conviction that the spirits protected their Home Islands, and that they would strike down any force that attempted an invasion, just as they had done throughout history.

Therefore, Operation Downfall was inevitable. And Cartwheel was the next phase.

The move by the forces through the central Pacific, primarily Navy and Marines but with some Army units, started in earnest in November 1943 with landings on Tarawa—a tough, costly lesson in which a total of 6,000 men died in a battle for an islet, Betio Island, roughly the size of New York City's Central Park—and then Kwajalein Atoll. After Tarawa, some immediately questioned the overall strategy. The cost was simply going to be too high if this was going to be the bloody outcome on every little atoll between there and Okinawa. But much was learned, including the value of underwater demolition teams and the mapping of underwater obstacles, such as reefs, to allow for easier landings. That would help with the Battle of Guam.

With the fall of the heavily fortified Japanese base in the Truk island group in February 1944, Operation Forager assumed even higher priority. Still, no one expected it to be easy to conquer the forces in the Marianas. The Japanese had held two of the primary islands, Tinian and Saipan, along with the smaller Rota and Pagan, since 1914, during World War I. They had continually bolstered their facilities there between the wars, despite international agreements not to do so.

Later, anticipating MacArthur coming back to attempt to retake the Philippines and an eventual attempt to invade the Home Islands, since 1942 the enemy had been building up defenses and troop strength in the Marianas, the Volcano Islands, and other locations in the region. The American military planners understood there was now a sizable force of experienced troops billeted on Guam for the express purpose of repelling any attempt to reclaim that island. They would be well dug in, too, just as they were on Saipan and Tinian and every island in the Pacific that the Allies had so far attacked.

The decision was made to first attempt a landing on Saipan on June 15 ("D-Day"—but this would be the other D-Day, since the more famous one in Europe had just begun on Normandy Beach a few days before). The thinking was that the United States would take on the most difficult objective first, and that would be Saipan. Also, Admiral Nimitz knew that airfields already existed there that, once the island was under Allied control, could be quickly converted by Navy Seabees to be able to accommodate the Superfortresses. As soon as the airfields were secure and modified, planes could be shuttled over from the Marshall Islands and bombing missions against the Japanese Home Islands could commence immediately.

No date was initially set for an assault on Tinian, and no plans at all were made for the two other enemy-occupied minor islands, Rota and Pagan. Guam would be the second objective, and the Marines were to launch their assault there almost immediately after the one on Saipan. The tentative plan was to send troops ashore on Guam on June 18 ("W-Day"), a mere three days after Marines first set foot on the beaches on Saipan. Everyone knew this timing was tentative at best. The exact date depended on how things went when those troops waded through the surf and trotted ashore on Saipan.

But then there was another major occurrence in the war, one that would unexpectedly delay the assault on Guam and any immediate end to the suffering of the Chamorros. It came even as the D-Day onslaught was in the process of being launched on Saipan. It would serve to keep troops that had been massed to invade Guam from even setting sail from their staging areas, while others already on the way would be diverted. Instead, they found themselves for the next several weeks fighting mosquitoes and boredom instead of Japanese troops.

Since World War I, the United States had been able to decipher most of the top secret Japanese naval code. Now it was clear from all the intercepted chatter that the Empire had no intention of allowing the Marianas to fall without an all-out defense. In addition to the thousands of troops based on those key islands, ready to fight to the last man for the emperor, the Imperial Japanese Navy (IJN) decided to send a powerful fleet steaming eastward across the Philippine Sea intent on taking on the U.S. Navy's Fifth Fleet, which was supporting Operation Forager. They would also attempt to deflect the troopships that they knew were delivering the Marianas Allied invasion forces from staging areas around the region.

Once that was accomplished—and the IJN was confident they had the carriers and aircraft to do it—they would go on to blunt the approach toward the Philippines by General MacArthur by preventing what they expected would be a major assault on the Caroline Islands. No one, and certainly not the Japanese, doubted MacArthur was on his way. The IJN was also certain that there would be a major attempt by the Allies to claim the rest of the Caroline Islands now that the United States controlled the former heavily armored islands of Truk.

The Carolines is an archipelago consisting of a wide scattering of small islands to the north of New Guinea. They were once a part of the Spanish East Indies. Today they are shared politically by the Federated States of Micronesia and Palau. However, in the spring of 1944, with the exception of Truk, Japan controlled them. And Japan was convinced the Allies would now try to use them as stepping-stones to all the other islands to the west, including the Philippines.

Crippling the Fifth Fleet and ending all attacks on the Marianas would surely prevent such an Allied move on the Carolines. Once they had halted these thrusts into their captured territory, the result would be a significant reversal in how the war had been going for Japan.

However, the reality was that there was no attempt under consideration by the United States commanders to take the Japanese bases on the widely distributed Caroline Islands. Not as a part of Operation Cartwheel. It was not part of plans for the upcoming Operation Forager, which involved ships and troops that might have been used in the Carolines if that had actually been considered. One of the results of the incorrect Japanese assumption would be the largest carrier-versus-carrier battle in military history. And the outcome would be the opposite of what the IJN had hoped for.

The Battle of the Philippine Sea on June 19 and 20, 1944, involved two dozen aircraft carriers and almost 1,400 carrier-based aircraft. It was a showcase for just how far the United States had progressed in the effectiveness of their carriers, aircraft, antiaircraft weapons, submarines, tactics, and training. American submarines torpedoed and sank two of the largest Japanese fleet carriers, while the U.S. Navy carriers launched hundreds of planes in wave after wave, sinking one light carrier and damaging many other ships. The battle was so one-sided, American pilots termed it "the Marianas Turkey Shoot."

As often happens in war, the ramifications of the outcome of the battle were not immediately known or fully appreciated. American commanders were initially disappointed, as they assumed they had missed a golden opportunity to wipe out most of the IJN. Analysis would later confirm that the "turkey shoot" had done sufficient damage to effectively prevent the IJN from having significant effect on the balance of the war. In addition to the carriers and other vessels damaged or sunk, the IJN had given up more than 430 carrier-based aircraft and about 200 land-based planes, most of which had come from the Marianas. They certainly would have been valuable assets to have to help defend against the American march through the islands over the coming months. And, of course, the Japanese lost hundreds of trained pilots and crew members with little means to replace either men or equipment. In all, Japan gave up about 90 percent of its carrier air groups in a mere two days under the almost continuous attack by American forces. Indirectly, this heavy loss also contributed to the adoption by the Japanese of a new and desperate tactic: *kamikaze* or suicide aircraft attacks.

That significant naval battle to the west of Saipan had no major ramifications on the scheduled date for the attempt to take the first of the Mariana Islands from the Japanese. Bombing and bombardment by battleships started hitting Saipan on June 13. The U.S. 2nd and 4th Marine Divisions and the Army's 27th Infantry Division, all under the command of Marine Corps lieutenant general Holland Smith, launched landing craft loaded with Marines and soldiers, going ashore right on time at 0700 on

June 15, four days before action started in full force in the carrier-to-carrier battle to the west. It would be July 9 and after almost a month of ferocious fighting before Saipan would finally be declared totally secure.

The United States sustained about 3,400 killed in action or missing and about 10,400 wounded on Saipan. The Japanese, however, lost 24,000 killed in action and an estimated 5,000 troops and officers who committed suicide, including all four of their highest-ranking commanders who were present on the island. In addition, about 7,000 Japanese civilians died, many of whom were also suicides, and an estimated 22,000 other civilians, mostly Chamorros, were killed.

Although it took a while, the fall of Saipan to the Allies, along with the enemy losses in the Philippine Sea, represented a staggering two-punch combination. Afterward, the prime minister of Japan, Hideki Tojo, resigned his office. Tojo, a former general in the Imperial Japanese Army, had been one of those pushing hardest prior to the war for a "preemptive" attack on the United States. He was convinced the destruction of the American Pacific Fleet—primarily the battleships—in an unexpected attack at Pearl Harbor would keep the United States out of the war, at least for the foreseeable future. That would allow the Empire to solidify its hold on the lands it had claimed already and build out still more military facilities while they claimed the Philippines, Guam, Wake Island, and other territory in China. And he had been able to convince a reluctant Emperor Hirohito of the validity of his theory.

Prime Minister Tojo was also responsible for policies that led to the harsh treatment of prisoners of war and the massacre and starvation of civilians in occupied territories. Now the resignation of Tojo was strong evidence that there might finally be a substantial fissure in the Empire's stone wall of resolve.

Meanwhile, W-Day, the date designated for the retaking of Guam, had been delayed due to the sea battle and the slow progress of the fighting on Saipan. Most of the invasion forces for Stevedore—Marines, Army, and Navy—had been assembled in March and April on Guadalcanal, a key island in the Solomons that had only been captured in February 1943 after six months of vicious fighting.

By mid-July 1944, the planning and logistics had long since been completed and in place. The timing seemed as good as it would ever be for W-Day to be rescheduled. Documents captured on Saipan indicated about 20,000 battle-hardened troops awaited the Americans upon their arrival on the sands of Guam. Those documents also confirmed the island was heavily fortified and well prepared to fend off an attack.

In addition to the anticipated concentration of enemy soldiers, the landing on Guam presented other significant challenges. Because of the reefs that surrounded the island and the imposing cliffs that made up most of the shoreline, there were only two good beaches, both on the west side of Guam—at Asan, near Agaña, and at Agat, south of Sumay and the Orote Peninsula—that could support the numbers of troops and then equipment that they would need to come ashore in each wave of the attack. It would have been virtually impossible to get tanks, trucks, and other equipment ashore while under fire at any other points around the island's perimeter.

Another issue popped up. Those two beaches were seven

miles apart. It would be unusual to send ashore that far apart two different forces that were part of the same operation. There had been no training for such a widely spread two-spear assault. However, there was no other choice.

Instead of the objective being to link up the two separate groups once they were ashore and had successfully established reasonably secure beachheads, they would, instead, plan on entrapping the Japanese between the forces like a giant set of pliers. It helped that intelligence indicated that the bulk of the enemy troops on Guam were well dug in between those two beaches, in the area previously occupied by U.S. Marines prior to December 1941. But it would be as obvious to the Japanese as it was to the American commanders that any major invasion would likely target those two points on the Guam shoreline. That eliminated any element of surprise.

By this time in the war, there were few surprises in how these operations might best be carried out. American forces had learned much from previous assaults on similar beaches around the South Pacific. The Japanese had changed little in their defensive tactics.

First, there would be the usual softening up. Initially, the U.S. aircraft would pounce, targeting troops, artillery emplacements, and fuel storage facilities, and attempt to catch aircraft on the ground. Next would be the wall of shelling and bombing from ships afloat as much as ten miles away. Ultimately, troops and equipment would come ashore in amphibious vehicles and attempt to establish a beachhead, then quickly push as far inland as they could support. That would allow the troops to dig in and prepare for a counterattack.

The enemy's first objective in previous assaults under similar conditions had been to stop the invasion forces before they even reached the beach, but that had mostly been successful only on much smaller islands and with air support. Here and on Saipan, the Japanese would have enough room and ample elevation from which to fire so they could create multiple lines of defense. They would certainly begin by laying down brutal fire on the landing troops while giving ground grudgingly. Artillery could also be put to use once the enemy knew which beaches would be utilized. If the Imperial Japanese Army could stop the invading force at the reef, they would not even have to defend the beaches.

By the time of Operation Forager, the Japanese knew it would be difficult to impossible to prevent a serious American assault from establishing some kind of beachhead. No American invasion force had thus far turned around and retreated back to their transport ships. Furthermore, the Americans were now employing some new amphibious landing vehicles that helped them tremendously in reaching the dry sand. The Japanese could only hope to take down as many men and neutralize as much equipment as they could during this phase of the assault, when the invaders were in the open and most vulnerable.

Then, just as they had done so often before in island assaults, the Japanese would attempt to stealthily break through the perimeter set up by the Americans while they were still in the process of digging in, with limited ammunition and their backs to the sea. While this typically failed, it did create a degree of chaos. That led to the next step, the surprise counterattack, usually launched in the dark of night, accompanied by renewed fire from machine-gun nests that the Americans believed had been abandoned. There would also be lethal artillery fire, well targeted, since the infiltrators from the earlier incursions would have determined where the greatest concentrations of the assault troops and supplies were located. The Japanese troops typically attacked openly, running, screaming, waving swords. With their daring charge and sheer numbers, quite a few would be able to run past machine guns and hastily dug foxholes, break through lines, and strike from behind or from the flanks. And they would launch these charges seemingly without regard for their own casualties.

Once such attacks failed—and they typically had, although such suicidal tactics had caused considerable loss of life for the invading forces, too—the Japanese would pull back to fortifications and caves in the mountains and jungles. From there they would make it a battle of attrition, again assuring heavy loss of life on both sides but postponing the inevitable.

As with other island invasions, the primary defense of Guam by the Japanese would almost certainly take place in the higher elevations and thick brush of the interior, and involve giving up ground a few bloody yards at a time. The Japanese still questioned the American will to conduct yet another frustrating, vicious, and bloody type of combat. The longer they could prolong the battle, the more the casualties mounted, the more men and equipment they could disable, the more successful the Japanese defense of Guam would be. The more time it would take and the fewer troops and assets the Americans would have available to move on to the next island up the chain.

To the Americans and to the Japanese, victory looked quite different.

Lieutenant General Takeshi Takashina, by this time the commander of the Japanese forces on Guam, also had the advantage of an additional month's warning that an invasion was imminent. A whole month to continue preparations. He made use of the time, employing the forced labor of the Chamorros to dig in—literally—and to get even better prepared for what he knew was coming his way.

He was right. The second objective of Operation Forager—W-Day—was still on the schedule, ready to be launched. But when? Once all forces were in place and poised, and after the tide had hopefully turned on Saipan, the new date for taking back the chunk of American soil was reset for July 25. But that was tentative at best.

The Battle of Saipan was the costliest to date for American ground combat forces in the Pacific. Finally, on July 9, 1944, at 4:15 in the afternoon, the commander of that portion of Forager declared the island to be secure. The top three Japanese commanders did not surrender, though. They all committed suicide in their cave headquarters.

The Japanese commander in charge of the naval aircraft and personnel on Saipan also killed himself when the outcome of the fighting became obvious and imminent. Vice Admiral Chuichi Nagumo was not just another air base commander, though. He was the commander of the main aircraft carrier group that conducted the sneak attack on Pearl Harbor. He had the same responsibilities at the Battle of Midway. Nagumo did not die in the usual samurai way, by disemboweling himself with his sword. He placed his pistol to his temple and shot himself. U.S. Marines would recover his remains.

Then, with the situation finally considered secure on Saipan, the date for W-Day was moved up. Instead of July 25, the Second Battle of Guam would begin on July 21. The assault on Tinian would occur beginning on July 24. Immediately, troops once again climbed aboard transports at various island bases and started toward the beaches of Guam. And the "softening up," the daily bombing and artillery bombardment, continued to mercilessly pummel the island but with renewed vigor.

Meanwhile, Navy radioman George Tweed mostly remained holed up in his vegetation-covered ravine hideout—really, more of a crevasse in the lava rock than it was a cave—on Antonio Otero's ranch. But the fugitive sailor was growing more and more exasperated. Several months before, with all the enemy soldiers combing the hills around his hiding place, he had been forced to leave behind many items, including his precious radio receiver and the generator to power it. He had given most of his possessions to islanders for safekeeping. Now he desperately wanted to know what was going on in the world. For all he knew, the Japanese had captured Los Angeles and were marching eastward toward Washington, D.C. He felt more and more cut off from the world, living a lonely existence in his dark underground bunker, coming out only occasionally for a bit of warmth from the sun or to get fresh air in the dark of night, when enemy patrols were not nearly as frequent.

Finally, and against his better judgment he decided to slip out one evening and try to retrieve the radio. Trusted friends, who still provided him food and medicine as best they could, strongly discouraged such a risky trip. They assured him that the Japanese were all over the jungle, digging their own caves and fortifications, hiding caches of ammunition and supplies, preparing for what everyone assumed was a looming invasion by the United States. They also reminded Tweed that roads had changed, buildings had been razed, landmarks such as trees and rock formations had been removed—mostly by bombs and artillery shells—and the trails he once knew had become overgrown, all while he was hiding. He could easily lose his bearings in the darkness or stumble right into the midst of one of the many enemy encampments that had popped up all over the island.

He had come this far. Why risk it? Some were also afraid that if Tweed should be captured and tortured, he might give up the names of some of those who had helped him. It was best that he remain in his isolated hideout in the jungle.

But George Tweed was tired of hearing the enemy version of the news that was being fed to the Chamorros. News updates in which the Empire always annihilated the Allies in every glorious victory. He obsessed over getting back that radio and regaining his lifeline to the world.

As he set out one night on the long hike, he was almost spotted by Japanese soldiers several times. As he had been warned, he got lost when his surroundings did not look the same as he remembered. Then, when he finally got to the home of the friend with whom he had left the radio, and after a nervous moment of greeting, he learned that the device was long gone, confiscated by the enemy, along with a bunch of Tweed's clothes and other items he was keen to get back. Even pictures of his wife and children.

The friend had been beaten viciously by the soldiers, who

tried to get him to reveal whether Tweed was still alive and where the American was hiding. The man did not know, and finally convinced the soldiers of that, as well as maintaining that a desperate Tweed had warned him at gunpoint, threatened to kill his family, and forced him to keep and conceal the items against his will. Eventually they believed him and allowed him to live. He was seriously injured during the interrogation, though, and it took him a long time to recover.

Now, here was Tweed, standing at the door of the man's house. Although the man was glad to see that the American was still alive, he urged him—begged him—to please be on his way.

Deeply disappointed, Tweed managed to make it back to his hiding place, bruised, bleeding, and with blisters on his feet. But just barely. He made it "home" just as the first rays of a new day illuminated Guam. Now, as he recovered from his venture out of the ravine, he realized the ordeal, the living conditions, and the limited food had made him even weaker than he thought.

Then, in mid-June, shortly after that dark, disappointing trek, the fugitive sailor was outside the ravine one day when he heard the unmistakable hum of approaching airplane engines. From the safety of thick foliage, he desperately tried to see the aircraft that were approaching the island from out over the sea. Hearing aircraft was not unusual. The Japanese had been bringing in plenty of planes lately, and they came and went all the time from the several airfields. But there was something different this time. He could tell from the sound of the engines that they were Americans.

Or was it merely wishful thinking?

Tweed would later proclaim that this day—Sunday, June 11,

1944—immediately became the happiest day of his life so far. His rescue was imminent. The Navy was coming back!

Carmen Artero was not very far away, several miles down the mountain from Tweed's cave, inside the little ranch house, which was crammed full of various family members. She, too, heard the approaching aircraft. But she thought little of it. She knew they were not Pan Am. She was now certain they would never return. She did not consider that they might be American airplanes. That this meant her misery of the last two years might soon come to an end.

Soon, even though the planes were above the clouds, there was striking confirmation that these were indeed U.S. aircraft, almost certainly off U.S. carriers. George Tweed heard clearly when they began dropping bombs. He heard the Japanese on the island unleashing a barrage of antiaircraft fire. He could then see fighter aircraft being launched to go after the attackers. The distant booming of the bombs striking targets on the ground was a beautiful sound to hear.

Then, even better, from his high observation position, the radioman could see columns of smoke indicating the explosives were finding their targets up and down the shoreline. That extended all the way down the coast almost to Sumay and the peninsula.

Tweed excitedly watched every day over the next several weeks as American planes roared in, dropped bombs, and strafed boats in the harbor and planes at the airstrip. Also, usually in the skies out over the sea, the Navy fighters took their toll of enemy fighter aircraft in dogfights. Sometimes, to his surprise,

92

the planes even attacked at night. Then the Americans flew away, only to be replaced by another wave of bombers, dive-bombers, and fighters.

That was wonderfully encouraging. The last time he had seen bombs falling on Guam, they had been aimed at him and his fellow sailors and Marines. Each day he hoped that this time the air attacks would be followed up by ship bombardments. And ultimately by wave after wave of troops storming ashore. He made sure he was up before sunrise each day so he could witness the landing, which would likely come around sunrise.

Each time, however, as day followed day and June turned to July, the incessant air raids seemed more and more like false alarms. They had been going on since mid-June, concentrating as expected on airfields and coastal gun emplacements and troop quarters. Then they would ultimately go away after un-leashing a couple of days' worth of mayhem. Another day or two would pass with no planes. On several occasions, a few ships had approached the island and lobbed shells in, but they quickly hustled out of sight again beyond the horizon.

But no troopships appeared. No amphibious craft approached the island, negotiating gaps in the coral reef. No massive bom-bardment was launched from distant ships. What was the pur-pose of all this softening up if there would be no invasion?

Tweed began to worry that there might not be an invasion after all. Maybe the Navy was just trying to keep the Japanese troops penned up on Guam while the Marines were busy cap-turing what they considered to be other more critical mounds of dirt and lava rock elsewhere in the Pacific. Surely they would not be softening up for an invasion over such a long period of time. Could it be possible that once again the Island of the Thieves was being forsaken? Considered not worthy of rescue?

From his position high in the hills—and he acknowledged to himself that it may have only been that he was desperately looking for something positive—Tweed was convinced the Navy flyboys and the occasional warship were taking a heavy toll, shooting enemy planes out of the sky and blowing up locations where he knew the enemy and their big guns were arrayed. He witnessed very few American planes going down.

What Tweed suspected, based on observations from one of the best vantage points on the island, turned out to be surprisingly accurate. From the day of the initial air strike by the United States against Guam until the first Marine stepped ashore, the Americans lost only sixteen airplanes. On the other hand, a significant number of fixed coastal guns—and plenty of coconut tree trunks disguised as guns—were destroyed.

Despite his elation at witnessing the air strikes, Tweed was quite worried about the safety of the Chamorros. Such an onslaught was certainly finding them, too. Word was that those who had remained in the towns had long since fled Agaña, Sumay, and other places when the American attacks began, finding spots to hide in the hills. He was hearing, too, of a dramatic increase in Japanese atrocities, senseless murders of innocent citizens who were suspected of acts of sabotage or simply showing the slightest hint of disloyalty to their occupiers and their emperor.

Then one day, as Tweed watched and waited for more of the

aerial show, he spotted something different going on out there on the horizon. It was a blur at first, far out to sea. A ship. Then there was another one.

He initially worried that they might be Japanese, bringing still more reinforcements to beat back any invasion. But as the ships drew a bit closer—maybe to eight or ten miles offshore—Tweed could tell these vessels were from the good old U.S. Navy. More and bigger ships than he had spotted so far. Battleships! Cruisers!

And as the warships lined up, broadside to the shore, he watched with growing excitement as their guns belched fire and smoke. There were now even bigger explosions all along the narrow strip of beach that Tweed could see from his vantage point. Pillars of smoke billowed skyward all up and down the west side of the island.

Over the next few days the warships regularly drew even closer. Some were new-design destroyers that Tweed had never seen before, and they boldly ran north, south, and back again, parallel to the west side of Guam. He had been isolated for more than two years now. It made sense that the Navy would have developed new vessels during that time. Sometimes he forgot that things might change even as time stood still for him in his sanctuary atop this ridge in the rain forest.

Tweed screamed with joy when he saw the ships, not caring if anyone heard him. What he had waited for, dreamed about, for two years and seven months was surely about to happen. If there were gunships standing off Guam, the long-anticipated invasion had to be coming very soon.

Finally.

Then Tweed forced himself to calm down. The time had come for him put into action the two-pronged plan he had considered as he lay in the jungle darkness and stared for days at the mossy walls of his cave.

First, he needed to do what he could to help the invasion force. He had plenty of valuable intel for them. Especially the locations of gun emplacements farther north along the cliffs. They had failed to take them out so far. All those ships and planes could target them, but that would make a landing easier.

Second, now that he was so tantalizingly near to the end of his own long nightmare, he needed to figure out how he could get rescued and taken off the island of Guam without being caught and killed.

CHAPTER FIVE

PIECES ON THE CHESSBOARD

The game of chess is an apt if overused metaphor for battle, primarily because it captures so well the distinctive characters involved and the methods they employ in attacking and defending. Clearly, the foot soldiers and sailors are the pawns, often sacrificed in battle in exchange for a tactical position on the board or the capture of a more important piece. The purpose of the game is to push the advance until the leader and his territory are neutralized. Only then can a winner be declared.

In the second battle for control of the island of Guam, there were about 60,000 well-trained American "pawns" on the board. They would be challenged by the 20,000 war-tested Japanese troops, deeply entrenched on their side of the board, awaiting all comers.

It could be argued that the pawns have a disproportionate effect on the outcome of a game of chess, partly due to their sheer numbers and the fact that they are typically on the front lines of the board in the early stages of the battle, when the strategy is initially executed. But it is certainly the more powerful pieces, the knights, rooks, bishops, queen, and king, who ultimately determine winner and loser. Or draw. When a gambit is employed, pawns quite often play a key part, even if they are not always aware of how they fit into the strategy. But it is those of higher rank who design and launch the attack.

The second battle for the island of Guam featured some of the most colorful and insightful power pieces of any clash of World War II.

At the top of Operation Cartwheel, with a new alignment that began officially on March 30, 1942, were the two key commanders of all Allied forces in the Pacific. U.S. Navy admiral Chester Nimitz was named Supreme Allied Commander—Pacific Ocean Areas. U.S. Army general Douglas MacArthur became Supreme Allied Commander—Southwest Pacific Areas. These two bigger-than-life characters did not necessarily agree on the best way to prosecute the war. Ego inevitably plays a role when men with such rank and power clash. And they tend to surround themselves with advisors who share their views.

As previously mentioned, MacArthur believed taking the most direct route through Japanese-held territory to return to the Philippines offered the best hope of breaking the back of the Japanese Empire. Admiral Nimitz was convinced island-hopping through the central Pacific, eventually taking the Marianas and the island of Formosa, would offer the best platform from which to interdict the shipping lanes to choke the Empire, and from which to eventually sortie forces to invade the Japanese Home Islands. The ultimate plan was a combination of both men's preferred proposals.

MacArthur began plowing ahead through New Guinea but with eyes always looking westward. Meanwhile, the island-hopping strategy of Admiral Nimitz did not get off to a very promising start. In November of 1943, Tarawa proved to be much tougher to capture than anyone suspected such a small plot of real estate would ever be. But with lessons learned from that episode, the Americans pushed on to successfully take Kwajalein, Roi-Namur, and Eniwetok. With the Marianas now in sight, Nimitz set his chessboard with strong knights, men who had gained great experience in a war that had by then been in progress for two and a half years.

Admiral Raymond A. Spruance was chosen as commander of the Fifth Fleet along with the Central Pacific Task Forces. That put him in charge of all units that would be sent to execute Operation Forager, the fight for the Marianas. Spruance was a native of Baltimore but grew up in New Jersey and Indianapolis, Indiana. He received an appointment to the U.S. Naval Academy from Indiana and was a member of the graduating class of 1907. His specialty was engineering, and he served during World War I aboard the battleship USS *Pennsylvania* (BB-38) as well as in the navy yard in New York City and, later, in Edinburgh, Scotland.

Between wars, he had considerable experience at sea, including commanding five destroyers and the battleship USS *Mississippi* (BB-41), and he held several engineering, intelligence, and

staff positions. He was described as a straight arrow who preferred symphonic music, never smoked, and rarely drank. Along
the way, Spruance had inherited the nickname "Electric Brain"
because of his calm, measured approach when faced with any
kind of challenge, small or big. He insisted on running a quiet
bridge aboard the ships he commanded. It was the same for the
war rooms where crucial planning for any action took place. He
preached that orders should always be issued clearly and con-
cisely. That, he maintained, was to minimize any chance for
misunderstanding or confusion. Ever the engineer, precision
was a priority.

Those traits would certainly show themselves when he commanded naval forces in two of the most decisive battles of
World War II, at Midway and in the Philippine Sea. Both sea
battles would be considered major Allied victories and significant turning points during World War II in the Pacific.

Even so, there were those who disparaged Spruance for his
execution of the latter, accusing him of not being aggressive
enough in the Battle of the Philippine Sea. With the benefit of
hindsight, they specifically maintained he should have chased
down and destroyed the escaping enemy aircraft carriers when
it appeared his fleet had them on the run and at their most vulnerable. After all, most of the Japanese aircraft, carrier- and
land-based, were now at the bottom of the sea. And with them,
their best-trained air crews were also gone. Without adequate
air cover, the IJN warships would have been easy pickings for
the American carrier-based planes.

In answer to his critics, Admiral Spruance would later point
out that he and his fleet had other more pressing matters to

attend to at the time. Matters that required their total attention and assets.

"We were at the start of a very important and large amphibious operation," he explained to naval historian Samuel Eliot Morison. "We could not afford to gamble and place it in jeopardy."

That amphibious operation, of course, was Forager, the invasion of Saipan and Tinian and the retaking of Guam.

Under Spruance, two other commanders would oversee each tine of a complicated and ambitious two-pronged attack on the key islands of the Marianas. Vice Admiral Kelly Turner, who had overseen naval forces for brutal landings at Guadalcanal and Tarawa, would command the Joint Expeditionary Force (Task Force 51), the primary invasion contingent set to go ashore in the Marianas. Turner would also directly supervise the units that were to invade and occupy Saipan and Tinian. That was the Northern Attack Force (Task Force 52).

The Southern Attack Force (Task Force 53), which included everything and everybody that would be headed for Guam, fell under the command of Rear Admiral Richard L. Conolly. He had overseen the invasion forces at Roi-Namur in the Marshall Islands.

Vice Admiral Turner had already seen his share of other ferocious action by the summer of 1944, including while serving in top staff positions and masterminding major assaults at Guadalcanal, New Georgia, Tarawa, the Marshall Islands, Roi-Namur, and Kwajalein. As it turned out, history has judged Turner for something else, his connection to two crucial missives, one positively, one negatively.

Turner was the commander who passed along one of the earliest and most accurate warnings of a potential Japanese surprise attack on Pearl Harbor. On the other hand, military investigators and historians would accuse him of not relaying other information that he later received related to an even more specific threat. Turner was accused of failing to alert the very commanders who would have been able to prepare the base and other elements of the Pacific Fleet for such a major assault.

On November 25, 1941, he had sent a dispatch to the chief of naval operations in Washington, D.C., telling him he had reason to believe an attack on American soil might soon be coming. Turner added, "I consider it probable that this next Japanese aggression may cause an outbreak of hostilities between the U.S. and Japan." President Roosevelt saw the message and insisted on softening the language considerably, most likely due to the sensitive nature of negotiations in progress at that time between Japan and the United States. Talks Roosevelt still believed could keep the United States out of the war.

The president made a guess, one that proved to be inaccurate, based on faulty intelligence from other sources. He was convinced that Thailand would be the Empire's target, not any U.S. territory. Japan, he felt, did not want the United States to enter the war. That modified version of Turner's message was the one that was passed along to other military leaders with no mention of an imminent assault on Pearl Harbor.

Later, though, Turner would be accused of not relaying to the commander of the Pearl Harbor base, Admiral Husband E. Kimmel, other intercepted Japanese messages that were even more precise and disturbing. Those dispatches strongly indicated that attacks were imminent. Whether he hesitated because of the previous disposition of his warning message or not, the apparent lapse regarding the second alert would be a stain that would mark the balance of Admiral Turner's otherwise impressive career.

Turner was noted for his furious temper and was nicknamed "Terrible Turner," even as he was also lauded for his command abilities. When Admiral Nimitz appointed him as commander of the Marianas assault force, he commented that Turner was "brilliant, caustic, arrogant and tactless—just the man for the job."

Major General Roy S. Geiger, a Marine aviator who had conducted the Bougainville operation, was set to directly command the Southern Troops and Landing Force, the III Amphibious Corps, for the assault on Guam. Like his counterpart for the northern Marianas assault, Lieutenant General Holland Smith, Geiger was a lawyer, holding an LLB degree from Stetson University in his home state of Florida. It is also interesting to note that Geiger enlisted in the Marine Corps as a private in November 1907. He scored so highly in a series of professional examinations and received such glowing reports from those under whom he served that he was offered a commission as a second lieutenant in 1909. At a time when military aviation was in its infancy, the Navy sent Geiger to Naval Air Station Pensacola in March of 1916 as a student aviator. He received the Navy Cross for action in which he led bombing raids in France during World War I. He then served in a number of staff positions between the two world wars.

By the time of Operation Forager, Roy Geiger was already a

decorated hero of World War II. He was awarded a Gold Star in lieu of a second Navy Cross for courageously leading a daring group of Marine aviators during the battle for Guadalcanal. His citation read, in part, "Major General Geiger's efficiently coordinated command succeeded in shooting down 268 Japanese planes in aerial combat and inflicting damage on a number estimated to be as great . . . Sank six enemy vessels, including one heavy cruiser, possibly sank three destroyers and one heavy cruiser, and damaged 18 other ships, including one heavy cruiser and five light cruisers."

Geiger had been asked to step away from aviation, though. He was charged with leading the I Amphibious Corps—a totally different type of chess piece—at the Battle of Bougainville. That unit was then redesignated III Amphibious Corps in April 1944, just in time to start preparing to go ashore on Guam. They would later see action on Palau. And Roy Geiger would receive two more Gold Stars for his leadership in both those battles. He would later command this same group when they went ashore—as part of the Tenth Army—on Okinawa.

Those with whom Geiger served maintained that he excelled in two very important areas: fire support by ships, aircraft, and artillery, and the less glamorous but vitally important realm of logistics. Each of those would prove to be essential in the effort to take back the island of Guam from a determined, well-entrenched enemy force.

Obviously, there are two sides involved in any chess match. The commander on the other side of the board, the head of that determined, well-dug-in force, was Lieutenant General Takeshi Takashina. A native of Japan's Chiba Prefecture, which includes portions of Tokyo, he graduated from the Imperial Japanese Army (IJA) Academy in 1913. He later attended the IJA Staff College, served on Formosa, and was an instructor at the Army Engineering College. Beginning in September 1940, he commanded the infantry group of the IJA 14th Division, stationed near the border of China and Mongolia. Soon after he was promoted to lieutenant general in October 1943, the IJA sent him to Guam. He was overall commander of the defensive forces on the island from early 1944 until the time of the American assault. His mission from the first day he stepped onto the island was to prepare to defend it from an invasion by the Allies.

Little else is known about Takashina other than that he was well schooled in the methods the Japanese had adapted for defense of the island territories in the Pacific: dig in deeply, oppose the enemy landing force, pull back, then, when the timing was right for maximum effect, counterattack viciously. And, if that fails, retreat, dig in even more deeply, and make the invaders pay dearly for every inch of ground taken. No surrender. Die at the hand of the enemy or commit ritual suicide.

Lieutenant General Hideyoshi Obata was Takashina's superior and overall commander of the Japanese forces in the Mariana Islands. His headquarters were on Saipan. However, he would unexpectedly become the direct commander of his troops on Guam shortly after that assault began.

Obata was the son of a Chinese language scholar, and that experience would serve him well in his later military career. In December 1911 he graduated from the IJA Academy, where he specialized in cavalry operations. Partly thanks to his language

skills but also due to military politics, Obata drew the assignment as a military attaché to the United Kingdom in 1923 and
then to British-controlled India in 1927. In 1938, after he was
promoted to the rank of colonel, he was reassigned from the
cavalry to aviation and became commandant of the Akeno
Army Air School.

Along the way, Obata married the daughter of Kageaki
Kawamura, one of Japan's highest-ranking and most decorated
military figures. Hideyoshi Obata's father-in-law died in 1926,
well before World War II, but not before being promoted to the
rank of viscount and becoming a field marshal in the Japanese
army. Those promotions were mostly based on his leadership in
the first Sino-Japanese War and the Russo-Japanese War in 1905.
Having a viscount as a father-in-law was likely an asset in Obata's military career, but he was also known as a tough, practical
leader.

In February 1944, Obata became the commander of the
Thirty-First Army, including the IJA's 29th Infantry Division
and 53rd Division. That put the veteran cavalry and aviation
officer in charge of defending the Mariana Islands against any
assault by the Allies, a daunting assignment indeed. He had already completed and put into place the plans for the defense of
the well-fortified island of Saipan, the assumed primary target
of any American attacks. But, as it turned out, he would not be
on Saipan to directly oversee the effort.

In one of the quirks of war, Hideyoshi Obata was away when
Operation Forager started. He was unable to get back to Saipan
and landed instead at the airfield on the Orote Peninsula on
Guam. The Japanese had assumed Guam would eventually be a

target of the United States but not necessarily an immediate one. Obata had every intention of getting back to Saipan when it was safe, when the island had been successfully defended, but, as it happened, he never made it. And his role in the Japanese defense of the Marianas was ultimately very different from what he had intended.

So it was that the game was set to commence, with all the pieces arrayed along and around a necklace of tropical islands on the western perimeter of the Philippine Sea. With the not-so-subtle reminder from Major General Geiger to his troops that "the eyes of the nation watch you," and with yet another admonition from Lieutenant General Takashina to his own troops, reminding them that each man had vowed to die in defense of this little peanut-shaped island, it was time for the opening move.

Technically, the American forces had already started the match back on June 11 when the first bombs fell on Guam. But the Marines set in motion the first major gambit just after sunrise on July 21, 1944. Although it would be most of a month before a checkmate, July 21 would become the date celebrated on Guam to this day as "Liberation Day."

CHAPTER SIX

W-DAY

The long-suffering Chamorros and the lone escapee remaining at large from the First Battle of Guam were not the only ones who had been frustrated by the lengthy delay of the American return to the island. In anticipation of the planned mid-June operation, thousands of troops were already on their way to Guam aboard transports transiting from Guadalcanal. They had been primed and trained to rush ashore and reclaim these 210 square miles of U.S. territory. Then word came on June 16 of the postponement of W-Day because of the intense action still taking place on Saipan and the massive carrier battle that was tying up many support vessels in the Philippine Sea. Upon the decision to postpone, the troop transport ships that were already underway changed course. They were directed, instead, toward the recently captured Eniwetok Atoll,

1,200 miles east of Guam, to await a new W-Day date there. It was a letdown for those on the ships, on Guam, and at other sortie locations throughout the region.

Meanwhile, unbeknownst to those who would engage in the eventual battle, a diplomatic move was afoot that could have stopped the invasion completely. On June 26, Emperor Hirohito instructed his foreign minister to contact the Allies and attempt to establish negotiations to try to end the war. Japan had lost much of its carrier naval power in the Philippine Sea. The defense of Saipan was not going well. Once that island fell, the Allies would have a much better platform from which to launch the B-29s with their devastatingly destructive capabilities. It had become obvious, even to Japanese civilians who only heard good news, that fuel, food, and other essentials were growing scarce and the importation of natural resources had fallen significantly. Shipping lanes were being constantly patrolled by American warships and especially by the highly effective submarines. The Allied plan to prowl those routes and starve Japan was now working well, further isolating the Home Islands.

The terms the Japanese sought in such peace talks would quickly be deemed unacceptable by President Franklin Roosevelt and his advisors. Now that the course of the war appeared to have turned in their favor, the Allies wanted nothing short of unconditional surrender. They certainly did not want Emperor Hirohito to remain as both titular and spiritual leader of the Empire, and that was one of the Japanese conditions.

Thus, the fighting would continue for another fourteen months, first for Guam and then ensuing tough and even more costly battles for Palau, the Philippines, Iwo Jima, and Okinawa. Taiwan would also be the scene of much air combat for the balance of the war but would not be invaded or captured in a ground assault. China controlled the island beginning in October 1945, after the end of the war.

With the emperor's peace proposal rejected, planning also continued even more determinedly for "Operation Downfall," the proposed invasion of the Japanese Home Islands, already tentatively targeted to begin in November 1945 and continue into early 1946. The estimate of the cost in human lives on both sides for such a mammoth effort, civilian and military, had already climbed into seven figures. And with each analysis, including the expected reclaiming of the Philippines and the climb up the archipelagos from the Marianas to Kyushu, the southernmost Home Island, the projected grisly count continued to escalate.

Finally, with the new date for the assault on Guam set, troopships and their escorts began departing Eniwetok on July 15. They would be followed by still more loaded transports over the next three days, from there and other islands. Those units originally on their way to Guam but redirected to Guadalcanal had continued to drill at length. They especially worked on how to best employ the newer amphibious landing vehicles known as "amtracs" or "LVTs" ("landing vehicles, tracked"), which could carry up to eighteen men.

Much had been discovered about the amtracs after they were first employed in the assault on Tarawa in the Solomon Islands. That had turned out to be a costly learning experience for the U.S. forces. Many of the amtracs had been caught on the atoll's reef, leaving Marines as little more than stranded targets for enemy gunners. Later, on the first day of that invasion, Japanese troops circled around under cover of darkness, climbed into some of the amtracs that remained stuck on the reefs, and set up their own machine guns. Then, at first light, they began peppering from behind the U.S. forces occupying the beachhead.

Now it was hoped that modifications and additional training would make the amtracs much more reliable and effective on Tinian and Guam. The coral reefs there would be a challenge. So would what they expected would be more intense enemy fire from the nearby cliffs. But planners hoped that Navy frogmen had blown usable gaps in the reefs and a high-tide assault would help assure they could get over them. They also hoped the training at sortie locations would dramatically improve their chances.

On Eniwetok and Guadalcanal, in anticipation of the Guam landing, troops especially worked on how best to cross reefs in the amtracs. Additional armor had been installed on them and made them heavier. They also trained at length on how to use the new 75mm howitzer artillery pieces that had been mounted on the vehicles. Those had already proved to be useful during the assault on Saipan.

The troops also experimented with another relatively new version of another vehicle specifically designed for beach assaults. Amphibious trucks (DUKWs), known as "ducks," were primarily created for bringing ashore artillery, ammunition, and other, less glamorous, but necessary heavy equipment and supplies for the fighting units already on the beach. These 2.5-ton, six-wheel workhorses were first used in mid-1943 in action in the Mediterranean Sea, and the newer versions had gone ashore a month before Guam as part of the invasion at Normandy Beach during D-Day in Europe. To enhance maneuverability and buoyancy, the ducks were not armored, but some did carry a .50-caliber Browning heavy machine gun in a ring mount for a modicum of self-defense. By the end of the war, several manufacturers had turned out a total of more than 21,000 of the vehicles.

Morale had been at a peak when the troops first left Guadalcanal for the planned June assault. But now, after the disappointing monthlong delay, the lengthy voyage to Eniwetok, the constant drilling and practicing, and then another protracted voyage to Guam from their staging areas, the troops were flagging a bit. But their spirits improved, as they were once again on their way to strike another blow against the enemy once their boots hit sand.

There were newcomers among them. Men who had not yet experienced battle. But a majority of the troops on the transports were veterans of previous action on similar islands. And they had survived. They had also shared their experiences and advice with the new guys.

At the time, neither the Navy, the Marines, the Army, nor George Tweed knew that the bombardment of the island of Guam had broken a wartime record. This had turned out to be the heaviest pre-assault softening-up salvo of any of the ones so far conducted during the war in the Pacific. The Japanese on Guam, as well as the civilian islanders, had also endured the bombing and shelling, which was ferociously long and intense. Deadly, too. Even though islanders had long since moved to places that were spared, far from military facilities, some of them still were unlucky enough to be in the wrong place at the wrong time. And while the Japanese were mostly sheltered in bunkers and caves when the bombs and shells fell, the ordnance still found some of the troops, with lethal results. A huge number of enemy aircraft had been destroyed or disabled over the few weeks prior to W-Day, and most coastal gun emplacements were now incapacitated. Towns along the western coast of Guam, including Agaña, Piti, Agat, and Sumay, had been decimated.

Still, the capable, well-equipped Japanese troops, all more than willing to die for their emperor, homeland, and ancestors, waited to engage the invasion force. As on islands already captured, the Japanese were adept at going deeply to ground, surviving the most intense hammering, then emerging from their holes to fight back ferociously. They were also experienced at hiding artillery and machine-gun nests in caves, crevasses, the jungle, and other spots that somehow escaped the pre-assault bombing and shelling.

Friday, July 21, 1944, dawned clear and dry despite the onset of the rainy season in the region. Downpours typically came daily, from mid-afternoon into the evening. The sea was unusually calm. At 5:30 a.m., with the sun not yet showing on the horizon, the U.S. warships—six battleships, nine cruisers, and a host of destroyers and rocket ships—began shelling the island with an even bigger barrage than had been typical for all those previous attacks. At first light, the fireworks became even more impressive as carrier fighters, bombers, and torpedo planes joined the fray.

The bombardment was hellish. The Japanese knew exactly what that meant.

Special underwater demolition teams had already visited the proposed landing beaches a week before, making detailed maps of the area to compare to piles of aerial reconnaissance photos. Then they returned to the appropriate beach approaches three days after that and destroyed hundreds of obstacles, including big blocks of cemented coral that Chamorro laborers had been forced to build and place strategically along the waterline.

While they were there, the U.S. Navy frogmen also left a sign at the edge of the surf for those who would soon follow them ashore: "Welcome, Marines. USO that way," with a prominent arrow pointing inland. Also, to divert the Japanese, the demolition teams had conducted a similar operation at Tumon Bay, farther up the shoreline, but without the USO sign. That included blasting boat lanes through the coral and marking them with buoys that could easily be seen by amtrac and duck drivers. Tumon Bay was five miles north of where anyone would be coming ashore, at least in the initial assault wave. Still, the activity would require the enemy to be prepared to defend that location as well.

Of course, the Japanese were aware of what the underwater demolition teams had done. And they also knew what that meant.

Many of the invasion force troops lined the rails of the ships that morning, watching the impressive fireworks show. They had already enjoyed the traditional Marine pre-landing breakfast of steak and eggs at about 3:00 a.m. The men were decked out in their fighting gear, with sheathed bayonets protruding from their packs. Many of them had been issued the bayonets only while they waited out the delay on Eniwetok. They smoked one cigarette after another as squad leaders moved among them, checking packs and weapons, encouraging them, but mostly nervously killing time until they were ordered to their landing crafts.

Aboard one of the ships, Major General Roy S. Geiger, the commander of the Amphibious Corps, stood with a microphone in his hand, impatiently awaiting the predetermined time when he would begin sending the landing forces ashore. Geiger was something of a military oddity, a Marine aviator—one of the very first—who rose to command an amphibious unit, as well as an enlisted man who quickly became an officer. But he had done this morning's chore before, the previous November at Bougainville, the largest of the Solomon Islands. There, after tough fighting, the Marines established a successful beachhead but, as part of the plan, made no attempt to capture the remainder of the large island. And even as Geiger stood there on that ship off the beaches of Guam with microphone in hand, fighting still raged at Bougainville.

Finally, Major General Geiger pushed the button and his voice spilled from loudspeakers aboard ships arrayed all around him. His words were carefully chosen and delivered with honest emotion:

"You have been honored. The eyes of the nation watch you as you go into battle to liberate this former American bastion from the enemy. The honor which has been bestowed on you is a signal one. May the glorious traditions of the Marine Corps' esprit de corps spur you to victory. You have been honored."

It was no accident that "honor" was mentioned three times in Geiger's short speech. Honor, courage, and tradition have been among the core values of the U.S. Marine Corps since its founding.

It was brutally hot already, and the humidity in the stifling, crowded well decks of the transports was insufferable. It was a relief for the troops when they were finally directed to get aboard their landing vehicles, where it would soon be marginally cooler. Most of them had done this before, too, on hot, steamy islands like the one that they could glimpse from the decks of the transports. After all the waiting, it now seemed as if everything around them was moving in slow motion.

That is, until the transport doors dropped and the tracked landing vehicles eased down their specially designed ramps, emerging into the first slanting rays of sunlight from beyond the island, the cool, fresh air, and seawater. Those who could see from the turrets of the amtracs were unable to make out the shore because of all the smoke and dust. It appeared a massive volcanic eruption might have occurred over there. And there was no sign of anyone shooting back at them from the island.

Suddenly, overhead, a flight of attack aircraft from the carrier USS *Wasp* (CV-18)—the planes as well as the ship were just back from the conflagration in the Philippine Sea—raced toward shore to further pave the way for the men who would soon be headed that way. The aim was for them to arrive at 0830, "H-hour," the specific time at which an operation or exercise commences. In this case, it was the time the first combat units were supposed to wade ashore and step onto dry-sand beaches.

The loaded landing craft circled, awaiting the final word. At about 0730, a flare went up into the brilliant morning sky. The sun had been up for about an hour by then. Rear Admiral Richard Conolly, the commander of the Southern Attack Force (Task Force 53), gave the simple four-word command: "Land the landing force."

The amtracs began their turn toward the beaches of Guam and an uncertain fate for each man aboard them. There was no doubt that many of them would not live to see the sun set behind them that night, out across the Philippine Sea.

Admiral Conolly turned to one of his staff standing nearby and confidently observed, "Conditions are most favorable for a successful landing."

The admiral had earned the nickname "Close-in Conolly" during previous action in the Marshalls because of his tendency to place ships delivering covering fire very close to the objective territory. Guam was no exception.

In total, the U.S. invasion troops involved in recapturing the island of Guam would eventually include units of the III Amphibious Corps, the 3rd Marine Division, the Army 77th Infantry Division, and the 1st Provisional Marine Brigade. By the morning of July 21, about 275 ships were in place around the island in support of those brave men.

It is also important to note that the cooperation between the Marines and the U.S. Army played a key role in action on Guam and the other Marianas. So often rivals, and prone to speak ill of each other, commanders of both branches of service would later remark about how well they worked together in this particular effort. The commander of the forces that had taken Saipan, Marine General Holland Smith—typically outspoken in his criticism of the Army—would glowingly refer to the Army 77th Infantry as the "77th Marines." That was high praise from a man nicknamed "Howling Mad" Smith and who was later relieved of command for his withering critiques of not only the Army but the Navy as well.

A battalion commander in the 3rd Marines also made comments that demonstrated the respect Leathernecks had for their Army counterparts in the Battle of Guam.

"In their fatigues so different from our herringbone utilities and their olive drab ponchos (ours were camouflaged) so different from us," he wrote, "there was no doubt in our minds that the 77th were good people to have alongside in a fight."

Among those young men now aboard amtracs pointed toward the two targeted landing beaches on Guam was a pair of Kentuckians. One of them, PFC Leonard Mason, born in Middlesboro, Kentucky, was a part of 2nd Battalion, 3rd Marines, 3rd Marine Division. He had been a Leatherneck for just over a year, having enlisted in April 1943. At twenty-four years of age, Mason had just been promoted to private first class back in March. As the first waves of landing craft began angling toward shore, Mason almost certainly thought about his wife, Donna, and his child, a two-year-old boy they had named Larry Eugene, waiting for him back home. And about his eleven brothers and sisters.

The other Blue Grass State Marine was twenty-one-year-old PFC Luther Skaggs Jr. from Henderson, Kentucky, a member of the 3rd Battalion, 3rd Marines, 3rd Marine Division. His buddies were already calling him "Tough Little Guy" because of his stature and how he always went about his duties directly, quietly, and with no complaint. Now, after seeing action on Bougainville, he would be a squad leader and rifleman with a mortar section of Kilo Company. That would assure he would have ample opportunity to again justify his nickname, just as he had previously in the Solomons.

On another of the LVTs was a Chicagoan named Frank Witek. His story was typical of many of the Marines approaching Guam that morning. Out of a sense of patriotism and outrage at Japan for the attack on Pearl Harbor—he had turned twenty years old three days after the Hawaii sneak attack—Witek immediately enlisted, more than ready to go fight and reap some revenge. It had not taken long to have both wishes fulfilled. He was sent to Pearl Harbor in January 1942 and saw action in several spots around the Pacific. His family heard from him once. He was in New Zealand then. He fought in three major battles in the first phase of the ferocious Bougainville Campaign beginning in November 1943. Along the way, the Marines promoted him to the rank of private first class. On Bougainville, he had served as a Browning automatic rifleman and drew duty as a scout, often behind enemy lines. Witek found himself with similar responsibilities on Guam, and that was perfectly fine with him.

Yet another Marine storming the island's beaches that July morning was a man who was not much older than the others with him in the amphibious landing vehicle. Yet Captain Louis Wilson Jr., at the ripe old age of twenty-four, was an officer, commander of Company F, 2nd Battalion, 9th Marines. Wilson's background was also different in some ways from those of the other three Marines, Mason, Skaggs, and Witek. Those young men were already in or likely headed for blue-collar careers before the Japanese attack on Pearl Harbor radically redirected the rest of their lives. Wilson, on the other hand, was already a college graduate before the war started. He also had plans for a career in the military even prior to World War II sending the other three men to enlistment offices. The Brandon, Mississippi, native had received his bachelor of arts degree from Millsaps College in Jackson, Mississippi, in May of 1941. There he was a member of the football and track teams as well as Pi Kappa Alpha social fraternity.

Louis Wilson had made up his mind to pursue a career as a military officer and did so by enlisting in the Marine Corps Reserve upon graduation from college. He was commissioned as a second lieutenant just one month before the war started. After the Japanese attack at Pearl Harbor, Wilson's reserve unit was activated and he was deployed to the Pacific theater, eventually serving with the 9th Marines at Guadalcanal, Efate, and, most recently before Guam, on Bougainville. Wilson was promoted to the rank of captain in April 1943.

When the sun rose on W-Day, as they prepared to go ashore with their brother Marines, none of these four young men—Mason, Skaggs, Witek, or Wilson—could have known that they would soon share another common bond. Each of them—three privates and a captain—would perform his duty with such valor that he would receive his nation's highest award for bravery, the Medal of Honor. Two of them would have the medal personally hung around their necks by the president of the United States. The other two would die on Guam and their families would receive their Medals of Honor posthumously.

Meanwhile, as the American assault was finally beginning, Lieutenant General Takeshi Takashina and his Imperial Japanese Army and Navy troops on Guam awaited whatever might be coming their way. They had been expecting the landing even before the first air attack by the Americans, and subsequent signs confirmed it was near. After all, the famous Tokyo Rose, in several of her radio broadcasts, had already told the Americans that their imminent attempt to reclaim Guam would have no element of surprise at all. She added that the effort was already doomed to fail and most of the Americans would perish before the rest would be driven back into the sea. The bravest and best trained Japanese troops awaited them. Plus, the islanders would be fighting right alongside the brave military defenders, each Guamanian willing to die to avoid once again being dominated by the American colonialists.

What Tokyo Rose said about Takashina having good defenders under his command was true. Many of his troops had only arrived on the island back in February, shipped in from Manchuria. They were well equipped with about forty tanks, plenty of ammunition, and well-placed bunkers and artillery emplacements—very experienced, and trained to defend against exactly the kind of assault they knew would be coming their way.

There had already been one serious setback in Japan's troop buildup for defense of the Marianas, though. A transport carrying 3,500 troops of the 18th Infantry Regiment bound for Guam had been sunk by the American submarine USS *Trout* (SS-202) on February 29, 1944, and 2,200 of the Japanese troops aboard were killed. Shortly after that successful attack, the *Trout* came under a particularly heavy depth charge attack and was presumed sunk, then later declared lost with all hands. That made her one of the fifty-two submarines lost by the U.S. in World War II. Eighty-one men went down with her—or, as the submariners say, "went on eternal patrol."

There had been other losses as well, mostly at the hands of U.S. submarines. That had mostly been supplies, ammunition, and, maybe worst of all, construction needs, such as cement. As it turned out, even with more than two years to prepare and plenty of warning in the summer of 1944 that the invasion was coming, the Japanese still had not been able to fortify as much as they felt would be necessary to successfully repel the invaders.

Technically, Lieutenant General Takashina was in command of both the army and navy defenders on the island. However, he had his immediate superior, Lieutenant General Hideyoshi Obata, looking over his shoulder throughout the invasion. Upon Obata's unexpected detour to Guam, he pointedly, and according to protocol, left to Takashina the conduct of Guam's defense.

As the early-morning barrage raged on, and with the U.S. Marines on their way, one Japanese officer addressed his men and attempted to further bolster their confidence: "The enemy will be overconfident because of his successful landing on Saipan. He has certainly planned a reckless and insufficiently prepared landing on Omiya Jima [Guam]. We have an excellent opportunity to annihilate him on the beaches."

The Japanese were possibly aware, too, that the U.S. Navy

had suffered its own significant catastrophe while preparing for the invasion of the Marianas. Though not as costly in lives, this one was even worse in some ways than the loss of the Empire's troop transport to the submarine USS *Trout*. The American catastrophic event was called by many the "second Pearl Harbor tragedy," or the "West Loch disaster," and it easily could have delayed the storming of Guam's beaches even more significantly.

In May of 1944, the West Loch area of Pearl Harbor was unusually crowded with vessels and the hustle of sailors loading them. The Navy was employing West Loch as the staging area for matériel bound for the Mariana Islands and Operation Forager. Twenty-nine landing ships, tank (LSTs) were tied up, berthed close together, all of them lined up along six crowded piers. The LSTs supported primarily amphibious operations and were designed to carry tanks, vehicles, cargo, and troops. They had the unique ability to take their cargo right up to a shoreline without a need for piers or docks.

At the Pearl Harbor West Loch facility, men loaded the ships day and night with munitions, fuel, vehicles, equipment, and more. It was specifically bound for the assault on Tinian and Guam. High-octane gasoline filled barrels that had to be stacked all along the piers because of lack of storage space. Each LST carried a crew of about 120 sailors and nearby were about 200 Marine loaders and support personnel. Most of those units were made up of African American sailors. None of them were experienced in handling such dangerous cargo and had not been trained at all for such work.

At about 1500 on Sunday, May 21, 1944, a massive explosion ripped apart one of the LSTs. More blasts followed almost instantaneously. The detonations could be heard for miles away and continued off and on over the next seven hours, into the dark of night. Many feared they were experiencing another Japanese sneak attack. More than 200 men were blown into the water by the detonations and twenty buildings were destroyed or heavily damaged.

Casualty numbers vary, but it is estimated more than 160 men died and almost 400 were injured. The Navy eventually declared the official cause of the tragedy to be a mortar round that somehow accidentally exploded, igniting the gas barrels. The lack of training of the men is generally considered by many who have studied it to be the primary reason for the disaster. That was never an official Navy or government determination, though.

In any case, the loss of six LSTs and all that ammunition, fuel, and equipment at such a crucial time could have been a serious blow to the Marianas Campaign. Yet, in one of the most concentrated efforts ever seen in one of the most unglamorous aspects of warfare, the load-out continued at an even more frenzied pace. The three-week delay in launching W-day allowed the Navy and many of the survivors of the massive fire and explosions to get replacement matériel to the West Loch piers, onto LSTs, and on the way across the Pacific to the location of the next phase of Operation Forager.

What Tokyo Rose had said about the citizens of Guam fighting alongside Japanese defenders was certainly not true. Once the initial American shelling and bombing began, many of the island's civilians had either found shelter at ranches, in caves, or grouped together in what they had begun calling "concentration camps." These were mostly rough lean-tos or tents cobbled together in jungle clearings or alongside streams. Life was extremely difficult for them. They had poor shelter, little food, no medicine, and limited clean drinking water. Many became ill. They did not attempt to hide from the Japanese but did all they could to conceal any food they were able to smuggle in, knowing it would be confiscated if the occupiers suspected they had it. Rations for the Japanese troops were growing scarce thanks to the U.S. Navy's blockade of the island, and the Japanese needed all the food they could find to keep the troops fed. The one thing they had in abundance, ammunition, was not edible.

By this time the enemy had become even more brutal in their treatment of the islanders, accusing the Chamorros of signaling the Americans, directing their aircraft and ship artillery to the best targets. There were reports of massacres of entire groups of islanders. Many disappeared, sometimes entire families, and were never heard from again. Others were penned up in camps, with poor food, little protection from the elements, and no medical treatment.

Sixteen-year-old Juan Cabrera and fifteen-year-old Beatrice Peredo Flores were among a group of people rounded up by the Japanese in Agaña and arrested for no good reason. They were marched into the hills and held prisoner in a cave for two days without any food or water. When they begged for something to drink or eat, they were screamed at and poked with bayonets. Finally, the eleven Chamorros—including Cabrera and Flores— were herded from the cave and forced to kneel at the edge of a crater, the result of a recent American bomb blast. On order, the soldiers used swords and bayonets to brutally stab their prisoners, shove their bodies into the crater, and leave them there, uncovered, for dead.

Although Cabrera had five deep bayonet wounds and Flores had all her neck muscles severed, they somehow survived the mass execution. Much later, in 1994, Beatrice Flores—at age sixty-five and, by then, Beatrice Emsley—testified about her ordeal before U.S. officials and in front of a congressional committee. She was doing so in support of the payment of war reparations for the people of Guam. Such reparations still have not been authorized by either the Japanese or U.S. government.

Antonio Palomo had vivid memories of his family joining five other families in a rough camp along a river, but far enough from the sea to hopefully avoid the intense shelling that had become an almost daily occurrence there. They used bedsheets and blankets as coverings against the monsoon rains. But when the American and Japanese aircraft conducted dogfights overhead, pieces of the planes would rain down on them, and Palomo remembered bits of them becoming caught in the sheets above their heads. They were able to see the U.S. Navy vessels as they appeared offshore, though, and that gave them hope that the troops would soon hit the beaches and liberate them.

Carmen Artero, eight years old by the time of the return of the Americans, would later recall the awful days when bombing and shooting from the ships and planes seemed ready to engulf the house at the ranch, including the big extended family now living there. The Japanese had also become even more hostile, taking families away to an uncertain fate. It was rumored that they had been tortured and then murdered. She knew her father, Antonio, was assisting the sailor who had been hiding from the Japanese for so long, and she still recollects how difficult and worrisome it was having to maintain that secret. A secret that had to be kept not only from the Japanese but from other islanders, just in case they might accidentally let something slip. Or have the information threatened or tortured out of them.

She still had vivid memories of the time when her mother baked a delicious cake, its wonderful aroma filling the ranch house. But before she and her siblings could even get a taste—a rare treat, considering all that was going on and the lack of ingredients—her father told them the cake was not for them, that he intended to take it to the sailor, Tweed. That was because the American had no food. The little girl cried and begged him not to take the wonderful-smelling cake away.

"Remember, Carmen," he told her. "We have each other, our family. That man has no one."

As the bombs and shells continued to fall, with an American landing pending, and with his meat store in Agaña long since demolished, Antonio Artero finally decided he needed to move the family to safer shelter than the house at the ranch. He chose to take them to the same mountaintop ravine where he had helped George Tweed remain hidden from the Japanese for the past two years. When they got there, Tweed was nowhere to be seen, although there were signs he had only recently departed. Artero reasoned that if the Japanese had captured him, it would be common knowledge among the islanders. He would have heard something. Chamorros were still being arrested and questioned about the radioman's whereabouts, even with the invasion obviously coming soon. He could only assume the sailor, and now good friend, had moved elsewhere on the island. That could be so he could meet the troops when they came ashore. Or perhaps try to get off the island and be rescued by the ships, the ones that came surprisingly close to the shoreline lately. Or maybe Tweed had moved and not told his friend, in order to protect Antonio and his family.

But even though Artero was worried about Tweed, he had another situation that was even more troubling. His wife, Josefa, was pregnant. Not long after they arrived at the rough hideout, however, she suffered a miscarriage. She was in danger of bleeding to death. Their only hope was that the Americans would finally come, quickly take back the island, find them, and give her medical assistance.

Antonio Artero correctly guessed where his friend had gone. George Tweed was no longer hiding there in the remote, hard-to-reach shelter he had built for himself in the lava rock crevasse. Several days before the Arteros arrived, the radioman noticed that American ships were daring to draw nearer and nearer to the coastline during their bombardment runs up and down Guam's western shore. There was some urgency spurring him to try to escape the island. The Japanese were all over the hills and jungles lately, digging holes, moving supplies into caves, building pillboxes, and sandbagging for machine guns and artillery emplacements. They had placed a big encampment only about a half mile from his lair. At night he could hear them singing, laughing, drinking sake. He knew it would only be a matter of time before they spotted him.

But he had an idea. He took some gauze bandages that Antonio Artero had given him, and, along with a pair of sticks, crafted himself a rough pair of semaphore flags. One problem: he had so rarely used this means of communication in his previous duty that he had forgotten most of the semaphore alphabet. He knew Morse code very well and could use a signal light, but he had only a shaving mirror for that purpose. He forced himself to remember as many semaphore letters as he could and then practiced for hours until his arms ached or until the makeshift flags fell apart.

Finally, convinced he knew enough to at least converse with a good Navy signalman on one of the ships—someone who could fill in the blanks for the letters Tweed could not recall—he put his plan into action. There was a spot he knew on a cliff overlooking the sea near Uruno Point, on the far northwest coast of the island. A place he often hiked before the Japanese invasion. There he began trying to attract the attention of the Navy vessels as they passed, first with flashes from his mirror and then with the signal flags.

Tweed was terrified that the Japanese might see him up there in the open, in broad daylight, and would come to get him. But he was also concerned that if they spotted him, they would realize on whose land he was hiding. That would mean certain death for Antonio Artero and his family in retaliation for harboring such a long-sought and valuable fugitive. One who could certainly signal information to the invasion force. Still, Tweed knew his best hope for rescue was to get the attention of one of the American warships and leave before an invasion.

Ultimately, he was able to do just that, communicating with a pair of destroyers that were operating especially close to the shore. Had it not been for Admiral Richard "Close-in" Conolly's practice of placing his covering warships near an assault objective, Tweed might never have been able to get anyone to notice him there on the bluff.

He would later learn that men on the destroyers had first believed his mirror flashes to be shots from the muzzle of a rifle. They assumed the Japanese were shooting at them despite the fact that they were out of range. They considered launching shells in his direction in response. But then they realized that what they were seeing was someone using a mirror, then some rough semaphore messaging. And that somebody over there was either friendly or had concocted a clever plan to lure the warship closer.

When one of the vessels finally acknowledged him, he hurriedly began to share information about a particular gun emplacement along the cliffs that was still working, one that could have been a real danger for the ships as they made their turn back to the south. He also told them that he knew about the location of enemy troops and other information that might be helpful during the softening up and invasion. He had considered that the Americans might believe him to be an enemy soldier or islander trying to entice the ships into an ambush. But he felt it was worth the effort and that, in his rudimentary way, he could convince them of who he was and what he was doing.

He was stone-cold certain of one thing: the ships' crews would not know who George Tweed was. Or who he once was. He had been a dead man for thirty-one months.

Somehow, with his flags and signal mirror, he persuaded the ships that he needed to be rescued and that he could be more help to them aboard than he could waving these homemade flags on a bluff. Although it was still daylight, and the American vessels were well within range of any guns that might be lurking along the shoreline, one of the destroyers dropped a motorized whaleboat into the water. Its all-volunteer crew brought the vessel close enough to shore so George Tweed could jump into the sea and swim out to meet them. The men in the boat kept their guns aimed at the skinny, hairy man frantically swimming their way.

Tweed was able to identify himself and briefly explain who he was, and finally, after all that time in hiding, he was picked up. Once he was pulled into the whaleboat, its crew turned back toward the destroyer USS *McCall* (DD-400), yet another ship just back from the victory in the Philippine Sea.

But Tweed stopped them. He had one more request. Despite his elation at being rescued and the real danger of remaining so near the island, Tweed convinced the whaleboat crew to take him back, this time much closer to the shore and the spot from which he had swum. That was so he could pick up equipment, pictures, and documents he had brought with him from his hideout. He did not want the Japanese to find it there, realize he had gotten away, and then, in retaliation, do something horrible to the Artero family.

The leery crew of the rescue boat relented and did as he asked, but always with eyes on the jungle and cliffs.

Once aboard the *McCall*, Tweed had much information to share about troop concentrations, defenses, and artillery and antiaircraft locations. And he also received a quick "battlefield" promotion to the rank of chief, along with a tally of how much back pay the Navy owed him. He would receive the money once he returned to the States. More than two years' worth.

Later, Tweed told everyone that he had one big regret. Once he was picked up, he was immediately taken away from the waters around Guam for debriefing, a shave and haircut, and medical care. Then he was quickly transported back to the United States for more interviews about his experiences, information that would be helpful in learning Japanese tendencies and tactics the Allies could use in upcoming island-hopping assaults. And with all the publicity in the media about his experience and rescue, he would also be tasked with making appearances and speeches, urging people to purchase war bonds, and exhorting factory workers to continue to turn out the materials needed to defeat the Empire. He was fine with all that.

But Tweed's big regret was that the quick exit from Guam meant that he would not be able to be an eyewitness to the one thing he had dreamed about for so long.

He would not be there to see the Marines storm ashore and snatch back the island from the Japanese.

★ CHAPTER SEVEN ★

H-HOUR

O n July 21, 1944, the Battle of Guam—to be accurate, the second one of World War II—was finally underway. This time, however, the fight was initiated by the United States of America to reclaim its own lost territory. At 0808, the amtracs designated to be the first wave of the 3rd Marine Division pulled away from the big group of circling LVTs and formed a well-spaced lineup 2,000 yards wide. Then they began to move toward the 2,500-yard-wide bit of crescent-shaped beach between Asan and Adelup Points—the "northern beaches"— located less than three miles west of Agaña, the island's most populous town. As part of the assault, the LVTs were accompanied by landing craft infantry, gunboats—LCI(G)s—each carrying about two hundred troops and armed with 4.5-inch rocket launchers.

The Asan beaches had been divided into color-coded sectors, left to right from the landing force's perspective, designated "Red 1," "Red 2," "Green," and "Blue." Each assault vehicle aimed for that segment of sand to which it had been assigned. The LCI(G)s headed for the flanks, aiming rockets at any point from which enemy fire seemed to emanate.

The bombardment from the naval vessels continued until the first amtracs and amphibious tanks were within 1,200 yards of the beaches. Then their aim switched so fire could be directed farther inland. The men could hear the ordnance from their support vessels screaming overhead as they moved toward their landing zones. At about the same time, scores of carrier-based fighter-bombers and over a dozen torpedo bombers made their final runs up and down the shoreline before shifting their attention as well to targets farther inland.

In addition to the duration and intensity of the pre-landing barrage, there was one other major difference in the Guam attack from previous beach assaults against Japanese-held territories. Other than the work of the frogmen blowing holes in coral northeast of Agaña, there was no attempt to fake a landing elsewhere to try to divert enemy attention and assets. Such tactics had been of little success in the past. Also, the logical landing sites on Guam were limited and obvious to everyone involved on both sides. It was hoped that the unusually large distance between the two actual assault points would be confusing enough to the Japanese that they would divide their attention and resources. Most of the previous Allied incursions in the Pacific had been against small atolls, often containing little more than an airfield, dug-in troop positions, and protective gun emplacements. Guam was much bigger, and the high mountains would be a challenge, especially in the early stages of the landing. From those highlands, the IJA could direct a variety of fire at the approaching amphibious craft, then troops on the shore, and eventually other motorized equipment and supply dumps. It was crucial the LVTs and LCI(G)s made it quickly through the reefs to the beaches and advanced promptly, disrupting those defenses.

Just before 0830, the first Marines had accomplished that first goal. They were on Guam at Asan. Meanwhile, six miles south of there and just a few minutes later, members of the 1st Provisional Marine Brigade came ashore on the southern beaches at Agat Bay, within sight of the Orote Peninsula to the north. There, thankfully, most of the coastal defense guns had been taken out during the bombardment and the Japanese had lacked the time, equipment, and construction supplies to get them going again.

Once the first waves of troops were on dry land on the northern beaches, they found that establishing a beachhead and advancing inland was going to be deadly difficult. The 3rd Marines were assigned the far-left flank of Asan Beach—Red 1—under the imposing Chorito Cliff, the highest knoll at the nose of Adelup Point. It had been misnamed on all planning documents as "Chonito Cliff," and even today is sometimes spelled "Chorrito." However, the men who fought at its base and along its steep incline would forever remember it. Enemy fire from that elevated position was withering. Landing craft returned fire, artillery from the ships was directed at it, and the Marines launched an attack on the area within an hour of hitting the beach.

No luck. The assault troops were either promptly pinned down or forced to fall back. They could not get close enough to diminish the fusillade. Directed air and artillery attacks throughout the day also failed to put a dent in it. As soon as the bombardment stopped, the resilient enemy were right back at it, raining hell down on the Americans.

Sergeant Cyril O'Brien, a war correspondent with the 3rd Marine Division, would make notes in his journal about the carnage: "Nearly half my old company lies dead on the barren slopes of Chorito Cliff. Four times they tried to reach the top. Four times they were thrown back. They had to break out of a 20-yard beach head to make way for later landing waves. They attacked up a 60-degree slope, protected only by sword grass, and were met by a storm of grenades and heavy rifle, machine-gun, and mortar fire.

"The physical act of forward motion required the use of both hands. As a consequence, they were unable to return the enemy fire effectively. Most of the casualties were at the bottom of the slope. They had been hit as they left cover."

The effectiveness of that one enemy position essentially prevented the troops on the northern beaches from advancing to the goal for the first day: the high point on the ridge beyond Chorito Cliff as well as the Fonte Plateau, another crease of high ground that ran from southwest to northeast, roughly paralleling the coast and overlooking Asan and Agaña. It was valuable territory to control if they were to start establishing along the landing zones reasonably secure dumps for ammunition, food, medical tents, and more that would be needed to support tens of thousands of tired, hungry, and wounded troops.

Other units landing on northern beach zones Green and Blue had to cross a series of exposed rice paddies while catching continuous fire from the ridges beyond. That made for slow progress as well, although it was not quite as fierce as the fighting at Red 1 and Red 2.

The headway made by the units who went ashore on the southern beaches was better. They soon pushed over a mile inland and secured the village of Agat—or what was left of it. But they were unable to extend their flanks as planned, due to terrain and enemy fire.

Back on the northern beaches between Adelup Point and Asan Point, Marine Company A, under the command of Oakland, California, native Captain Geary R. Bundschu, had finally battled their way to within a hundred yards of one of the enemy emplacements that had been causing so many problems. It was a well-camouflaged concrete blockhouse near the nose of the point—it was later found to have a reinforced four-foot-thick roof, explaining its seeming invulnerability—and it was pouring out machine-gun and small-arms fire along with shells from 75mm and 37mm guns. The infernal barrage had already taken out several amtracs, some before and others just as they reached the shore.

Bundschu's guys were determined to neutralize the bunker, but they were taking heavy casualties in the effort. The captain got on the radio and requested permission to pull back and regroup. The request was denied. His commander simply did not want to give up ground so dearly won. So, instead, Bundschu requested corpsmen and stretchers.

As it turned out, Company A and others trying to reach the deadly bunker would remain there at that position for almost fifty hours, exposed and vulnerable. Some of the troops had only clumps of grass to hide behind. Mortar shells launched by the enemy from somewhere beyond the summit landed among them off and on, all night long, both nights. The Japanese on the ridgetop tossed grenades out and allowed them to slide down the steep bluff, right into the holes where some of the Marines were dug in, waiting for daylight.

But their captain would not be there to see them through the two long, awful nights. Late on W-Day, at about 1700 hours, Bundschu's Company A and other units attempted an all-out charge to the promontory. Again they were kicked in the teeth and thrown back. The last fifty feet below the enemy installation was nearly vertical. The attackers had to grab onto roots and scrub bushes to keep from tumbling back down the bluff.

During that desperate charge, Captain Geary Bundschu was killed. The captain posthumously received the Navy Cross for his valor that afternoon on the bluff. His citation reads, in part, that Bundschu "reorganized his men in preparation for another fierce assault against the Japanese-held ridge. Although his right arm was rendered useless by a grenade fragment when his platoon was caught in a hostile machine-gun crossfire and simultaneously subjected to a vicious grenade attack, according to his Navy Cross citation, Captain Bundschu courageously directed his men to take cover then, valiantly pressing forward [and] succeed[ing] in destroying the nearest Japanese machine-gun position with grenades before he was mortally wounded."

Captain Bundschu's story includes one of those odd twists that often occur during war. His maternal grandfather, Thomas J. Geary, had served as a member of the U.S. Congress from California. In the late 1800s, Congressman Geary introduced a piece of blatantly discriminatory legislation forbidding Asians from being allowed to become American citizens through naturalization. Though targeted primarily at Chinese, the law specifically barred the Chamorro people of Guam from being able to earn citizenship.

There is more irony associated with the story of Captain Geary Bundschu. The only geographical feature on Guam named for someone who fought on the island in World War II is Bundschu Ridge. The name of a brave young Marine captain who gave his life to help rescue the Chamorros. That name had been given the ridge by commanders aboard one of the ships when they heard news of the captain's death. It stuck.

Upon their initial landing, the 21st Marines took the center of the northern beach, while the 9th Marines were responsible for the right flank, nearest Asan Point. They all faced brutal fire from the higher elevation ahead of them. But with the help of tanks, one company did get to the ridge along Asan Point, helping clear the way for the 9th Marines. Those units were then able to move so quickly that they had to purposely slow their advance to avoid leaving defenseless gaps in the lines.

With one other exception, the going was far from easy anywhere else along the two landing zones. The 21st Marines happened upon two gorges—called "defiles" in military terms—that ran straight down from the top of the ridge. They were surprised to find that neither was guarded. The men were able to climb quickly to the top of the ridgeline and then keep a watch on the defiles to allow other troops to climb up them as if marching up stairways.

That was in stark contrast to the barrage faced all day by the 3rd Marines on the left flank of the northern beaches. Those units caught the worst of the Japanese resistance. From the time they climbed from their landing craft, the Marines were under intense artillery and mortar fire from the cliffs above them. The terrain offered almost as much resistance as the enemy. In addition to rolling hand grenades down the cliff face, the enemy defenders had snipers hidden all along the rough landscape, protected by vegetation. They had a relatively easy time picking off any American who dared raise his head. Even after the sun went down, the Japanese continued firing rifles and mortars at random and dropping the grenades among men seeking shelter in darkened, hastily dug foxholes.

Meanwhile, tanks and other equipment arriving ashore were encountering their own issues. Mines had been buried in the sand. And there were many traps and ditches that had been dug to make more difficult their push away from the unprotected beaches and deeper into the island.

As darkness fell late on W-Day, Private Luther Skaggs was one of those Marines who were settling in for the night, determined to defend the precious ground that they had managed to claim so far, even as the enemy continued to crush them. Earlier in the day, as they waded ashore, his section leader had gone down only steps away from Skaggs when a mortar round struck nearby, gravely wounding the man. Skaggs checked his leader's condition, saw he was already gone, then took charge of the platoon. He led his buddies as they eventually advanced about two hundred yards inland through the heavy fire, claiming a strategic spot, one they hoped to hold on to for the night and then, with first light, use it to launch an attack on the deadly enemy positions at the top of the ridge.

During the night, though, one of those hand grenades falling down the cliff from above landed in Skaggs's foxhole, lodging there. There was no place to go. When it exploded, it shattered the young Kentuckian's leg. Somehow, all alone, Skaggs was able to apply a tourniquet to stop the spurting blood. Then, ignoring the agonizing pain, he managed to prop himself up against the wall of the foxhole. He kept fighting, shooting at enemy troops, tossing grenades when any of them came close enough to his position.

Skaggs never called a corpsman or complained. Although some of the members of his section were nearby, they had no idea he had been seriously wounded. They heard him fight for more than eight hours. Just before daylight, he told the others to continue fighting until they reached their objective. He then crawled out of the foxhole and dragged himself back toward the rear to seek medical attention.

Against his wishes, Skaggs was transported to a hospital ship waiting offshore for treatment. He would eventually recover but ultimately lost the mangled leg. The war was over for the "Tough Little Guy."

As the sun came up on day two, and not far away from where Luther Skaggs was crawling back toward the beach, Private

First Class Leonard Mason, his fellow Kentucky native, found himself and the rest of the 2nd Battalion Marines under sudden devastating fire. The platoon had finally begun to make some progress, wiping out lingering positions to allow them to try once more to reach what they had planned as their first day's goal. The men were working their way up a gully when they almost stumbled into the middle of an enemy machine-gun emplacement, equipped with two weapons, not fifteen yards away from them. The Marines hit the ground just as gunners in the bunker opened up on them.

Pinned down, under fire from above, there was no hope for them to get away. In a minute or two, enemy mortars would zero in on them. Suddenly, Mason climbed out of the gully and began quickly crawling through the thick brush, trying to work his way around behind the enemy emplacement. He took fire, not only from the machine gunners but other riflemen in the jungle farther up the hill. Bullets struck his arm and shoulder. Undeterred, Mason pressed on, to a spot where he might be able to do some damage and silence the Japanese weapons. But he was again hit, this time by a burst of machine-gun fire.

Though critically wounded this time, Private Mason refused to stop. He somehow managed to raise his rifle and fire multiple times into the machine-gun nest, killing five Japanese soldiers and critically wounding two others. The two enemy guns were out of business, no longer a threat.

Finally, in intense pain and bleeding badly, he slid back down the hill to where his platoon remained dug in. Mason informed them of what he had accomplished. Only then did he give his consent to be evacuated and seek treatment for his wounds.

It was too late. Those final injuries proved to be fatal. The war was also over for PFC Leonard Mason. He had died to save the lives of his fellow Marines and push the fight against the enemy.

It would be late on W-Day plus one before the Marines would finally reach the top of Chorito Cliff, eventually taking the enemy positions from behind. Most of the Japanese troops had pulled back by then, disappearing into the thick jungle. Thanks to the heroic work of men like Skaggs and Mason, the original goal of the assault on the north beachhead at Asan was finally achieved. It was a costly and temporary victory. The enemy had only moved deeper into the hills and would continue to defend the higher ground even as they likely prepared for a counterattack.

Meanwhile, on the south beachhead at Agat, the 1st Brigade did not face anything as formidable as the terrain at Asan. Still, they were finding enemy resistance growing more intense due to troop concentrations in the area as well as impressive pre-constructed fortifications. As on the northern beach, this area had also been broken into four sections by the invasion planners. Here, the descriptive names were not quite as colorful: "Yellow 1," "Yellow 2," "White 1," and "White 2." The beach and land nearby were pocked with pillboxes and other fortified shelters for warriors and weapons. The Marines were finding that some of the defensive positions had somehow escaped the attention of photo interpreters during the planning of the assault. Not a single bomb had touched some of them during the massive and prolonged pre-assault barrage.

The unseen guns suddenly and unexpectedly came to life. While the initial amtracs, tanks, ducks, and other craft were approaching, little to no enemy fire had come from the beach. But then the guns in the untouched blockhouses started clattering and booming, along with fire from many other emplacements, just as the assault wave crossed the reef and hit sand. In addition to the carnage, the loss of the amphibious vehicles would prove costly. After delivering the first wave of troops, and once the beach was secured, they were set to transport more men, ammunition, and supplies from boats offshore and across the reef to Agat. Not having those assets would prove to be a problem for days to come, including the assault on Orote Peninsula. Troops on the southern beaches had already run low on ammunition even before the tropical sun had set on W-Day.

As they had used the natural ridges, cliffs, and ravines to mount a defense at Asan, the Japanese employed man-made resources to defend against the invaders at Agat Bay. They had used island labor to construct thick-walled bunkers and pillboxes that had not been dented in the least by the vicious pre-assault bombing. Those structures, along with the blockhouse guns and still more machine guns that had been placed on a small island nearby, meant the troops had come ashore under a lethal crossfire.

Even so, the 4th Marines were able to establish a beachhead on the right flank, then moved quickly across low ground to set up on the road that ran to Agat from the inland mountains. This was especially important. From assaults on Guadalcanal and other enemy-held islands in the Pacific, the Marines knew the methods the Japanese typically used. Fight viciously. Make certain every inch of sand is hard-earned and blood-soaked. Next, stealthily pull back, but then filter back down from the hills, usually under cover of darkness. Probe for weaknesses in the American lines. Get behind them and attack from the flanks and the rear. Then, with confusion at its maximum, come with the counterattack.

It was dispiriting and the cause of much uncertainty. Just when the Marines felt they had captured and secured territory, the enemy would be not only in front of them but all around them, coming at them in the darkness from all directions, screaming like banshees. When they did, they were clearly willing to die.

As expected, the enemy troops that had been manning the trenches along the beach had melted back into the jungle and gullies, but they still kept up heavy mortar, sniper, and machine-gun fire. Despite that, and mostly because of superior numbers, the Marines reached one of their initial goals on the southern beaches—a thousand yards inland—by 1035 on the first morning.

Other units had taken heavy initial casualties on the southern beaches but were reaching their objectives by late in the afternoon of day one. A command post had been set up on the beach, the town of Agat was secured, and the Orote Peninsula had by all appearances been cut off, all by late afternoon. Despite that, everyone knew that plans to eventually claim the peninsula against so many enemy troops would be extremely difficult.

Regardless of the progress, not all had gone perfectly during the southern assaults, either. Casualties were high. One group of Marines, responsible for securing the center of the beach at Agat, had quickly and easily reached their initial 1,000-yard objective and were moving on to the next point when American shells from ships offshore began falling short of their targets. The Marines were forced to stop their advance and pull back to avoid annihilation by friendly fire. Then, about midday, enemy shelling zeroed in on the battalion aid station that had just been established. Members of the medical team as well as wounded troops were killed or hurt, and precious medical supplies were destroyed. It would be late the next day before a replacement doctor for that post could be brought ashore.

As night fell on Guam on W-Day, an African American Marine unit, the 4th Ammunition Company, was assigned to guard the ammunition depot on the south beachhead. It would be a long, sleepless, and potentially disastrous evening. During the night, the Marines intercepted and killed more than a dozen infiltrators, each strapped with explosives, determined to blow up the dump.

On the Marines' first day back on Guam, they had pushed inland by just over a mile in several places. The one glaring exception remained the northern beach in the shadow of Chorito Cliff near the town of Asan. There were a few breaks elsewhere in the line, too, and especially a two-hundred-yard gap at the gorge through which flowed a branch of the Asan River. The towns of Asan and Agat as well as Bangi Point, which poked out into the sea just south of Agat, had been cleared except for a few stragglers harassing with small-arms fire. The Marines had a tenuous foothold on the face of the Fonte Plateau, another area of higher ground six hundred feet above sea level and just over a mile from the beach. They had hopes of capturing that high ground after daylight on day two.

It had been pricey territory. The division had lost, at best estimate, 105 men killed in action, 56 missing, and over 500 wounded in the first eight hours of fighting. That number would certainly increase during the dark tropical night, as casualty counts continued. But commanders acknowledged that it could have been worse had the assault not advanced as quickly as it had. By the time the enemy pulled back from their beach positions and set up mortars and artillery deeper into the island's interior, the Americans had already pushed ahead and started digging themselves in.

Several commanders noted, though, that every time the Marines moved ahead and cleared a ridge, they found more enemy soldiers on the other side of it. That, however, would soon prove to be a harbinger.

Lieutenant General Takeshi Takashina was assembling the bulk of his forces beyond the Fonte Plateau in preparation for a major counterassault, one he believed could drive the superior American forces off the high ground they had captured already and ultimately shove the invaders back into the sea.

A counterattack of any significance, though, would come only if Takashina was satisfied that he could eliminate the maximum number of American fighters without sacrificing too many of his own severely outnumbered troops. His preferred plan was to continue a battle of attrition, defending higher ground while keeping the invasion forces at bay, unable to claim the island or begin to build airstrips for their bombers, then launch a counterattack when the Americans were confident they had the Japanese forces beaten.

The Americans were already building airstrips on Saipan and Tinian. Even if Takashina ultimately lost the island, he would have slowed the U.S. advance through the Pacific, reduced the capability for the brutally heavy bombing on the Home Islands, and removed as many American troops from the war as he possibly could. For that reason he was hesitant to order an all-out counterattack on any large scale this early. In a few days, yes. Just not now.

Yet one of Takashina's commanders was convinced he could do just that, and on the first night, by attacking the Americans in the darkness, elbowing them off the recently captured high ground of Hill 40 and the beach beyond, all the way back into the Philippine Sea. All he needed was his commander's permission.

Before the sun went down on July 21, he was on the field telephone with Takashina, seeking just that.

Captain George McMillin, commander of the naval forces on Guam and the island's military governor in December 1941, when the island was invaded by the Japanese

The Government House on the Plaza de España in Guam's capital, Agaña, before World War II

Waves of troop carriers approach the beaches of Guam on W-Day, July 21, 1944.

Marines approach the northern beaches in a transport (a landing vehicle, tracked, or LVT) during the initial wave of the attack.

Marines leave an LVT and scramble for cover in the early stages of W-Day, the beginning of the Second Battle of Guam.

Troops seek shelter on one of the northern beaches under withering Japanese fire.

Shells aligned on the deck of a battleship, ready to use before and during the assault on Guam

Marines advance inland on Guam from the southern beaches.

LVTs line up along the beach as the area is secured.

A Marine machine-gun nest. Note the bombed-out jungle in the background.

An American flag is erected on one of the secure beaches as a Marine hangs a communications cable in a coconut palm nearby.

U.S. troops enter the captured town of Agat near the southern beaches and the Orote Peninsula.

Troops of the 3rd Marine Division rest after clearing Agaña.

Marines with a captured Japanese soldier

A flamethrower is used to burn out a Japanese pillbox on the Orote Peninsula.

Members of the 1st Dog Platoon patrol on Guam. The animals were a great asset to the U.S. invasion forces.

Marines help a wounded comrade to an aid station.

Troops display a plaque recovered from the former Marine barracks on the Orote Peninsula. The barracks had been a key objective of the Japanese invasion on December 10, 1941.

Marines accompanied by Sherman tanks advance on the last enemy positions on Guam.

Top commanders of Operation Forager gather on Guam after the island is declared secure. *Left to right*: Admiral Chester Nimitz, General Alexander Vandegrift, Lieutenant General Holland Smith, and Major General Roy Geiger.

CHAPTER EIGHT

HILL 40 AND FONTE RIDGE

A s the sun fell into the sea on W-Day, assessment reports rolled in to the American commanders. Plans were confirmed or altered not only for the coming night but for first light on day two. The first job was to hold ground against certain counterattacks. It was especially crucial to hold high ground for its tactical advantage in protecting the beaches, where more men, ammunition, and equipment continued to stream ashore.

One important point was an area listed on planning maps as Hill 40, to the right (southwest) of the landing forces on the southern beaches at Agat Bay. Units of the 1st Battalion had immediately encountered blistering defense from the elevated ground near Bangi Point as they waded ashore, even though the area had been inundated by shelling and bombing for days. It looked more like a moonscape than tropical jungle. That was the first indication that the Japanese valued the hill. After it ultimately fell to the Marines, the importance was confirmed by a deep cave system dug into the back side of the headland. As with other points along the higher ground above the beaches, the enemy had tunneled in deeply there, only to emerge after what was assumed to be devastating bombing, still able to throw down a wall of fire once Americans hit the beaches below.

It ultimately took troops from the 3rd Battalion and tanks to kick the enemy off Hill 40. Now that they had it, they would have to defend it.

Other units had pushed inland across lower ground and numerous rice paddies, all the way to Harmon Road, one of the island's vital highways. This route was critical to maintain in U.S. possession, as it provided a way to transport men, tanks, and other equipment wherever they were needed up and down the coast, and eventually to roads leading to the inland mountains. It could also offer a valuable artery for a counterattack, too.

One of those inland mountains was Mount Alifan, southeast of Agat. At about eight hundred feet above sea level and with even taller mountains behind and to the south, it was a perfect spot for the command post of the Japanese officer who led the enemy's 38th Regiment, Colonel Tsunetaro Suenaga. From there, he was convinced that he could dive down upon the tired invaders as they tried to get organized and quickly overpower them. Suenaga dialed up Lieutenant General Takashina on the field telephone at about 1730 on the first day to plead his case and ask for approval to make his move during the coming night.

Takashina reluctantly agreed. He still favored waiting a day or two before staging the counterattack, but he also knew the advantages of hitting the invasion force before they could settle in and better equip themselves. But just in case, he was explicit in his order that survivors of such a counterattack—if there should be any—were to fall back to Mount Alifan and once again await the American advance.

At around 2130 that night, about 750 Japanese troops attacked Hill 40 from the south and east. Others managed to find and exploit gaps in the lines and quickly advanced toward the two beaches. It was a typical Japanese attack, and many of the U.S. commanders and Marines had seen it before. Colonel Suenaga aggressively pushed his men hard. Hundreds died. American flares and star shells from the ships offshore illuminated the attackers, making them easy targets for machine gunners. Colonel Suenaga himself led the attack on the right flank, troops with rifles held high, screaming as they charged, tossing grenades into every hole in the ground as they raced past.

Based on their previous battle experience, the Marines managed to hold off firing back as the enemy raced toward them. Then, when the time was right, they finally opened up on the wildly charging adversaries. Even so, some Japanese broke through, still tossing hand grenades and bayoneting Americans in their foxholes. Multiple bullet wounds appeared to leave the counterattackers unfazed. They seemed unstoppable.

One entire company of enemy troops penetrated to an area

near the regiment's command post on the southern beach but were eventually fought off. All of them were killed by the next morning. Another Japanese unit made it to Harmon Road, along with four tanks, and began moving quickly toward the beach. They might have driven all the way to the beachhead had it not been for Private First Class Bruno Oribiletti and his bazooka. He bravely knocked out two of the tanks, sent enemy soldiers diving into the ditch, and stopped them in their tracks long enough for the 4th Marine Tank Company to show up and destroy the other two tanks. Oribiletti died in the fight. He later received the Navy Cross for his bravery. Another large unit of enemy troops stumbled right into the area in which the newly arrived 305th Infantry was still in the process of establishing a perimeter. All the Japanese eventually went down in heavy combat.

Fighting continued until dawn. Every man of the 750 Japanese soldiers who charged Hill 40 died. So did practically all the rest of Colonel Suenaga's 38th Regiment. Suenaga himself was wounded, continued to fight, but was again struck and this time killed. The failure of the attack on Hill 40 also left the considerable contingent of Japanese troops on the Orote Peninsula isolated and surrounded. They would have to fend for themselves. The trepidation of Lieutenant General Takashina had proven to be well-founded.

The few survivors of the ill-fated enemy counterattack limped back before daylight to join the troops who were preparing to defend Fonte Plateau. Among them was Shoichi Yokoi, the would-be tailor and now loyal supply sergeant from Aichi Prefecture. Somehow he had escaped the slaughter surrounding him during the long night, had inflicted damage on the invaders, and would live to again fight for his emperor and ancestors.

The Marines had suffered significant casualties, too, but by turning back the charges all along the perimeter that first night on Guam they had prevented potential disaster. Lieutenant Colonel Alan Shapley, commander of the 4th Marines, later stated, "If the Japanese had been able to recapture Hill 40, they could have kicked our asses off the Agat beaches."

Although Marines had scaled part of Fonte Plateau relatively early in the assault, the high ground now posed the next major obstacle to the forces on the north beaches. The area designated by planners as Fonte Plateau actually included a swath of relatively level high land above Asan Bay. The ridge ran from the main spot that carried the name—at an elevation of 617 feet above the sea, offering a great view of the Asan beach all the way to the Orote Peninsula—to Mount Mangan, a mile to the west. Today, a portion of this area is known as Nimitz Hill.

Marines who had fought, won, and lost tough battles on other islands had already decided that Chorito Cliff and Fonte Plateau provided by far the roughest terrain they had faced to this point in the war. It would take two full days and the lives of more than six hundred U.S. Marines—including Captain Geary Bundschu—to finally take Bundschu Ridge. And once the troops got there, they found the enemy had mostly just vacated the area. The few troops who remained resisted to the point of suicide.

Meanwhile, down below them, other Marines marched toward and successfully secured the town of Piti, where the U.S. Navy base had been located prior to December 8, 1941. They encountered some resistance but they, too, found mostly abandoned enemy positions.

Another contingent moved to take Cabras Island, a long, sandy stretch of land near Piti. The primary obstacles there were thick patches of briars, numerous snipers, and thousands of land mines. Clearing the island gave the Marines a perfect point from which to observe both Orote Peninsula and the northern beachhead. It also allowed them to put guns in place to accurately fire on the peninsula once the inevitable assault there cranked up. That and allow some of the Marines to catch a bit of a rest.

A young Marine from Texas, Raul Escobar, had turned eighteen years old on the troopship bound for Guam. He would later remember his time on the island as "hell. I can't describe it any better." He had already had his fill of death and danger. But he would also describe how he and his fellow Marines would help relieve the horrible tension with their homebrew alcoholic mixture. They would mix raisins, apples, and apricots, hide it in the dirt from their superiors, and then imbibe after it had had time to ferment. They called the recipe "raising jack."

"We had our good days and our bad days," Escobar would later say.

As the Marines prepared to thrust into the highlands, the primary concern was that the various units had not yet hooked up and secured a solid perimeter. The terrain, and especially the deep gorges, made it problematic. Through day two and three, they made every effort to shore up, but some areas, where vegetation was limited, left deadly open ground that was constantly raked by machine-gun, mortar, and sniper fire from even higher ground farther inland. Enemy guns were frustratingly well hidden within clumps of trees and especially in the deep ravines. They were almost impossible to spot from ground or air. That kept the Marines pinned down, unable to advance or close ranks with other units to their left and right.

Major General Geiger knew that they had not yet encountered the bulk of the enemy troops on Guam. He was also certain the Japanese were not that far up the hill from the broken perimeter his troops were struggling to establish. And he was dead certain his adversaries would eventually stage a counterattack much more lethal than the first night's assault on Hill 40 and the southern beaches. That made it even more crucial that the Fonte Plateau be taken so forces from both beaches could reconnect and prepare for the next steps in securing the island.

The fighting on July 25—W-Day plus four—was as vicious as any since the first day and night of the invasion. By the end of the day, a unit of Marines had gouged their way through the enemy lines and seized another important objective, the Mount Tenjo Road, within a few hundred yards of the high point of Fonte Plateau. But the men were in an exceedingly vulnerable position. They were finally joined near dusk by another group who had spent the day blasting and using flame throwers on enemy caves. The two units quickly prepared to launch an attack to claim the ridge, a fight that would certainly be at close enough quarters that most casualties would be from point-blank small-arms fire.

That was exactly what it turned out to be. One of the leaders for the Marines was Captain Louis Wilson, the Pi Kappa Alpha fraternity brother from Mississippi. He was commanding officer of Company F, fighting to get to the top of the ridge in near hand-to-hand combat. Wilson was wounded three times. His eventual Medal of Honor citation described well the amazing bravery and sheer determination Wilson demonstrated during the ferocious encounter:

"Ordered to take that portion of the hill within his zone of action, Captain Wilson initiated his attack in midafternoon, pushed up the rugged, open terrain against terrific machine-gun and rifle fire for 300 yards, and successfully captured the objective. Promptly assuming command of other disorganized units and motorized equipment in addition to his own company and one reinforcing platoon, he organized his night defenses in the face of continuous hostile fire and, although wounded three times during this five-hour period, completed his disposition of men and guns before retiring to the company command post for medical attention. Shortly thereafter when the enemy launched the first of a series of savage counterattacks lasting all night, he voluntarily rejoined his besieged units and repeatedly exposed himself to the merciless hail of shrapnel and bullets, dashing fifty yards into the open on one occasion to rescue a wounded Marine lying helpless beyond the front lines. Fighting fiercely in hand-to-hand encounters, [Wilson] led his men in furiously waged battle for approximately ten hours, tenaciously holding his line and repelling the fanatically renewed counterthrusts until he succeeded in crushing the last efforts of the hard-pressed Japanese early the following morning. Then organizing a seventeen-man patrol, he immediately advanced upon a strategic slope essential to the security of his position and, boldly defying intense mortar, machine-gun and rifle fire which struck down thirteen of his men, drove relentlessly forward with the remnants of his patrol to seize the vital ground."

Not all the fighting that day on the Fonte Plateau involved rifles, pistols, and bayonets. During the afternoon of July 25, four tanks shuttled up Mount Tenjo Road. Captain Wilson's executive officer, First Lieutenant Wilcie O'Bannon, slid down the slope to meet them and point out potential targets. The tanks blasted away. They then used their radios to summon naval fire and assure there would be star shells lighting up targets during the upcoming night. The tanks had also brought welcome ammunition, including hand grenades.

By dawn the next morning, an estimated 600 Japanese had been killed. Yet there were other counterattacks as mentioned in Captain Wilson's citations. The Japanese were just as relentless as expected. It would take another two days, until July 28, for the plateau to be declared captured. In the effort, the Marines lost 62 men killed in action and about 180 wounded.

As it turned out, deciding that any bit of ground on Guam had been cleared would often come back and bite the Marines. Die-hard enemy troops would suddenly appear as if from nowhere, popping up in the middle of territory believed to have been secured. Four days after the initial landing, one group of Marines was surprised by an unexpectedly large squad of Japanese that had been hiding in caves on the eastern branch of the Asan River, not far at all from the beachhead. Again it was close-quarters fighting and repeated attacks before the enemy were ultimately wiped out. No one could figure out how that many adversaries could have remained undetected for four days and nights before suddenly appearing and attacking.

Even bigger and more perplexing attacks were soon to come, however. In the late-night darkness of July 25 and into the early morning of July 26, just as a heavy rain began to fall, there was a sudden massive counterattack against the Americans from an almost supernaturally determined group of Japanese. This was the counterpunch that Lieutenant General Takeshi Takashina had planned all along.

As the Marines fought off those screeching, charging troops hurtling their way at a full run, they suddenly realized that there were still more enemy who had worked their way behind them. And they were taking a toll. They had somehow gotten past the well-established perimeter, most likely by using ravines and the beds of small streams as passageways down which they made their way to near the beach. By doing so, they had made good use of the worrisome gaps in the Marine lines, too.

One commander reported his men were relaxing, trying to stay dry under their ponchos during a welcome lull in the fighting but in the midst of a tropical rainstorm. A trained Labrador retriever—an asset of the 1st Dog Platoon and one of sixty canines that were an integral part of the Guam operation—suddenly sat up in his handler's foxhole and began whining.

The handler sent the word. The enemy were coming.

It started with probing attacks and quickly escalated to a full-scale banzai charge by a stunning number of enemy troops. It was clear the attackers had been nearby for most of the night before the resting troops suddenly felt the full force of the charge. It came at most points along the perimeter at about 0430. Some of the attackers appeared to be inebriated. Indeed, earlier that day, advance scouts had spotted Japanese troops drinking. Their loyalty to their emperor and willingness to die had apparently been bolstered by bottles of sake.

After they were able to beat back the ghostly aggressors with the help of mortar strikes and vicious fighting, the commander could see just how close the enemy had been before the strike. Three of his dead had succumbed to bayonet thrusts, most likely during the initial probing.

At other points, the various perimeter gaps that had been of concern to Major General Geiger and other commanders allowed many of the Japanese to get past the American lines. One group infiltrated a point to the left of the 9th Marines and launched a rather disorganized attack. They wildly charged ammunition and supply dumps, artillery emplacements, and even tanks. It appeared the ammunition and supplies were their primary targets, but they still tried to kill every human being they passed while striving to reach those objectives.

A group of about two dozen infiltrators managed to make it all the way to where medics had set up a hospital just off the northern beach. When the Japanese began charging with their usual bloodcurdling screams, doctors hurried to get the more critically wounded onto stretchers and evacuated out of the back of the tents to hide in the vegetation. Everybody else, including cooks, corpsmen, and less seriously injured men, grabbed rifles and started shooting at the shrieking, storming Japanese.

Help quickly came in the form of two companies of the 3rd Pioneer Battalion. It took them more than three hours to repel the enemy. The defenders eventually killed three dozen Japanese. Only one patient was wounded but the 3rd Pioneers lost three men.

The next morning there were reports from all along the western side of Guam of terrifying action during the long night. Men told of enemy troops materializing out of the misty darkness, charging in droves, tossing hand grenades, hacking at men with swords and machetes. But when the sun finally rose on July 26, and with the hard-won Fonte Plateau solidly in the hands of the American forces, the initial phase of the assault could be declared completed. Now it would be possible to combine forces and advance farther inland, especially to the north and east. That would have been near impossible without the capture of the plateau.

Based on the best counts available, the Japanese appeared to have lost about 3,500 troops in the one night's attacks. Even more costly, that included almost all the officers who led those strikes. The Americans were confident about 95 percent of the enemy officers died within the first three days of the assault on Guam. It was estimated that about 300 U.S. troops died and about 200 had been wounded.

It fell upon Lieutenant General Hideyoshi Obata, on behalf of the direct commander of Guam's Imperial Japanese Army forces, to report the failure of the bold but desperate attempt to push back the American forces. He was also obliged to apologize for it and renew his pledge to defend Guam to the death. Obata's dispatch to IJA headquarters in Tokyo said, in part: "On the night of 25 July, the Army, with its entire force, launched the general attack from Fonte and Mount Mangan toward Adelup Point. Commanding officers and all officers and men boldly charged the enemy. The fighting continued until dawn, but our forces failed to achieve the desired objectives, losing more than 80 percent of the personnel, for which I sincerely apologize. I will defend Mount Mangan until the last by assembling the remaining strength. I feel deeply sympathetic for the officers and men who fell in action and their bereaved families."

The cryptic reply from Imperial General Headquarters commended Obata and the troops for their sacrifice but urged them to prolong the fighting on the island as long as possible as part of the ultimate defense of the Home Islands.

Now there was one primary obstacle left to overcome along the crucial middle of the island's western coast. That was the concentration of Japanese troops on Orote Peninsula, estimated to be about 5,000 men. A number of them had tried to emerge from the finger of land to join the previous night's attempt to push the Americans back to the beaches. Many had died in the process. But there were still thousands of well-trained, well-equipped fighters dug in there, waiting for the American charge.

The plan had been to attack Orote on W-Day plus one, but the difficulties securing the beaches, the constant firing from the higher points inland, logistics issues (the beaches at times had resembled knotted-up rush hour traffic), and the vicious counterattack the night of July 25 into the twenty-sixth had slowed things down.

Orote was vital. It was the location of the former barracks for the small contingent of U.S. Marines who had been called upon to defend the island two and a half years before. The site of one of the island's most iconic structures, the Pan American Hotel. The location of the town of Sumay. Home to the island's best and longest airstrip. But most importantly it was the strategic point that would have to be cleared of enemy warriors in order to finally gain safe access not only to the landing strip but to Guam's only deepwater harbor at Apra.

What was left of the ferocious enemy troops there would certainly fight to the death to protect this strategic neck of land. And they had been preparing to do just that for more than two years.

★ CHAPTER NINE ★

CHARGING A TANK WITH
A SAMURAI SWORD

By July 25—four days into the Second Battle of Guam—the 22nd Marines had fought their way north from Agat. It had been a hard-won couple of miles. They had reached the isthmus, the narrow point, that connected Orote Peninsula to the rest of the island. Meanwhile, the 4th Marines had managed to secure the approximately eight-hundred-foot-tall Mount Alifan, which overlooked the southern landing beach and also offered a good view of Orote. What had once been the command post for Japanese colonel Tsunetaro Suenaga and the 38th Regiment was now abandoned after their first-night debacle. Now the U.S. plan was to place a noose around the throat of the highly valued peninsula and draw it tight.

The observers peering in that direction from the recently

captured mountain could see a strong defensive force dug in and waiting. Then the U.S. barrage began. Artillery from the 77th Infantry Division began pounding spots up and down the five miles of sand, scrub, and swamp, from the isthmus at the east end to Guam's westernmost tip, Orote Point, at the other. With no enemy planes in the sky, antiaircraft guns were used to concentrate fire on the southern side of Orote. Other emplacements just set up on sandy Cabras Island pummeled the north shoreline.

One of the first chores for the artillery came early on the morning of July 26 when enemy troops on the peninsula tried to break through the line established by the Marines to join in Takashina's counterattack. As with other Imperial Japanese Army troops, these came in a chaotic and deafening charge. According to one estimate, more than 26,000 shells were concentrated on the attackers between midnight and 0300. Tanks fired at almost point-blank range. Still the enemy fighters kept coming, as if possessed by demons.

The Marines fought back valiantly and were finally able to repel what was left of the charging enemy soldiers. There were more reports about some of the Japanese appearing to be almost falling-down drunk. Several enemy officers were observed charging tanks, waving samurai swords, screaming at the tops of their lungs, as if challenging them to a very one-sided fight.

Another group of enemy troops on the peninsula made an attempt during the night of July 25–26 to climb aboard and launch barges, then float them across Apra Harbor to join the counterattack. They were chased back to the peninsula by gunfire from U.S. Navy ships and the troops on Cabras Island.

When dim daylight finally illuminated the mangrove swamps on the morning of July 26, more than four hundred Japanese troops—many dismembered, having been blown apart—were being pounded once more, but this time by heavy rainfall, forming puddles reddened by blood.

The advance onto the peninsula was set to begin early on the morning of July 27. As the Marines began to make their move, they could see human body parts hanging in the few surviving scraggly trees. Between the monthlong softening up and the artillery storm since the day before, the peninsula looked as if it had been stomped by some giant herd of stampeding cattle. Surely nobody could have survived such a horrific pummeling.

But as the Marines began the assault, they barely made it the length of a football field before a hailstorm of small-arms and machine-gun fire sent them belly-down into the mud. Then, almost immediately, artillery opened up from somewhere on the peninsula as well as from behind, from the mountains, shells falling amid the Marines as they scrambled for cover. They waited until after 0800 to resume the charge, this time with the aid of tanks and some well-placed mortar rounds.

But the next obstacle was not provided by the IJA. It was the thick mangrove swamp, still full of Japanese. The only way through was a narrow, two-hundred-yard pathway, wide open to enemy fire. The troops had to work their way slowly, mostly on their stomachs, alongside tanks, which directed fire over their heads into pillboxes and sandbagged machine-gun nests.

It was after noon before most of the men made it through that bottleneck. Other battalions farther north had easier terrain to negotiate onto the peninsula, including what was left of the main roadway to Sumay, but they had to deal with equally vicious gunfire. And almost continuous rainfall.

While some units made maddeningly slow progress, others pushed deeper, almost to the old Marine barracks and rifle range, where the island's brave Insular Guard—at least, the ones with rifles capable of firing—had once practiced, preparing to resist an enemy invasion. But just as some units seemed to be moving quickly, they would suddenly encounter a cluster of well-dug-in enemy gunners or a stretch of open ground littered with lethal land mines.

One group of Marines watched with interest as a Japanese officer suddenly stepped from cover and charged a tank, swinging his sword in a broad circle above his head. The tank gunner did not hesitate: he cut the officer down. It was clearly a form of ritual suicide, something the American troops would see in abundance over the next few hours, days, and weeks.

The Marines were also surprised to see whole groups of enemy troops suddenly climb from their hidden, well-defended bunkers and run away wildly toward the west end of the peninsula. Speculation was that they feared the artillery would start up again, paving the way for the invasion force. But that allowed the Americans to move to within three hundred yards of the barracks and the airfield. Securing those objectives, however, would not happen until the next day.

As American forces inevitably moved westward and prepared for the final push—by late on July 27 the enemy would hold only the west quarter of Orote Peninsula—they made sure they cleaned up behind themselves. Demolition crews blew up scores of elaborate bunkers and rough holes in the ground.

Flamethrowers torched others. Too often Japanese soldiers had emerged from "destroyed" bunkers and killed American Marines and soldiers.

At daylight on the twenty-seventh, an artillery and air bombardment lasting an hour and fifteen minutes had crushed the remaining enemy-controlled areas. Then the Marines drove toward the airfield, Sumay, and the barracks, starting at about 0830. The rain had let up a bit, but it was still muddy and oppressively hot. Somehow, though, the Japanese held on, stubbornly spitting out machine-gun and rifle fire, even with their backs to the Philippine Sea, with still more artillery likely to cut loose on them if they persisted, with a far superior force streaming their way, and with little hope of pushing the Americans back.

Frustrated at the slow going, the higher command ordered an infantry attack, supported by tanks, beginning at 1530. But even then the Japanese showed they had no intention of easily giving up this little bit of real estate, and would sooner go to meet their ancestors than allow the Americans to move in. Night found the Marines within view of their objectives but still unable to get to them without serious sacrifice. They would wait. The end to this part of the story was inevitable. But the primary objectives were still two nights and a day from being secured.

After the usual wake-up artillery barrage and a massive air strike on the morning of July 29, W-Day plus eight, and with Army and Marine tanks leading the way, the airfield and barracks were finally secured. Resistance by then was almost nonexistent. The assault forces gave credit to the big guns and aircraft for convincing the enemy to finally give way.

But many of the Americans witnessed things they would never forget. Groups of Japanese soldiers plunging off cliffs to certain death. Others stepping into the open, inviting bullets. Or pulling the pin on a hand grenade, then dropping to the ground to curl up around the device before it exploded. Others cut their own throats and then sat there quietly as they bled to death. Some of the Americans felt sympathy for the enemy. Maybe more so for their families, who lost a dear one for what the Marines saw as such a senseless cause.

Among those killed during the action on July 28 was the commander of the Japanese forces on Guam, Lieutenant General Takeshi Takashina. He was struck by fire from a machine gun on an American tank as he tried to rally surviving troops off the Fonte Plateau and into hiding in the jungle beyond. Takashina had served his country and its emperor for more than thirty years. His son, Takehiko Takashina, was also an officer in the IJA, and after the war he would eventually rise to the highest rank of any officer in his country's postwar military.

Now, with Takashina lost, his direct superior, Lieutenant General Hideyoshi Obata, the man who had been stuck on Guam when he was unable to return to his headquarters on Saipan, assumed command of the remaining troops defending the island.

Although the Orote Peninsula had not yet been totally cleared of enemy fighters, a heavily symbolic flag-raising ceremony was held at the old barracks on the afternoon of July 29. A captured Japanese bugle was used to play "To the Colors." It was not lost on anyone that retaking one of the few bits of ground ever surrendered to an invader by the United States was something to be properly celebrated. The island of Guam had been in enemy hands and its population virtually held captive for thirty-one months. Brigadier General Lemuel C. Shepherd Jr., the commander of the 1st Provisional Marine Brigade, made a short speech to the weary troops at the ceremony, declaring where they now stood to be "hallowed ground." Shepherd assured those men able to gather around for the event that they had certainly avenged the loss of their comrades who had died when the Japanese came ashore on Guam in 1941, "overcome by the numerically superior enemy three days after Pearl Harbor." He proclaimed that the island would remain "as an American fortress in the Pacific."

At least there on the peninsula things began moving rapidly from that point onward. Engineers were already at work clearing the airfield of debris and skeletons of aircraft, and repairing bomb and shell holes in the runway. They made quick work of it. Less than six hours later, a U.S. Navy torpedo plane had to make use of the runway to attempt an emergency landing. He was successful.

After bodies were counted, the assault force determined that taking Orote Peninsula back from the Japanese had cost the brigade 115 men killed in action, more than 700 wounded, and 38 troops remained missing. The enemy had lost more than 1,600 men.

One thing had become obvious: while many enemy soldiers had died in the two major fights on Guam so far, there were far more that were still not accounted for. Only about one-third of the known troop strength had been killed or captured. None could have escaped the island. That meant there was still a considerable force of enemy warriors who would fight to the death to keep the Americans from capturing Great Shrine Island.

Once the happy flag-raising ceremony was over on Orote, American forces could now be combined. They would begin to move north and south, to the higher elevations and into the thick tropical forest, ferreting out the enemy wherever they might find them. The experienced Marines had a pretty good idea of what the next few weeks would involve, and none looked forward to it.

It would be dirty work. Dirty and deadly.

CHAPTER TEN

A PAINFUL COST

One of the next challenges of the Battle of Guam would be a surprisingly large contingent of enemy troops in the crotch between Mount Alutom and Mount Chachao, due east of Apra Harbor. Achieving the tops of both points of high ground would require displacing the enemy units there, and there was only one way to do it: with brute force. The commander of the 3rd Battalion of the 9th Marines called in an artillery barrage, then followed with a swarming attack, mostly using bayonets, grenades, and, when his men had the opportunity, their rifles.

When the dust settled, 135 Japanese lay dead and the rest had melted back into the rain forest. From these mountains the Marines could now see their U.S. Army infantry counterparts atop Mount Tenjo to the south. They all had good views of the beachheads from Agat to Agaña. The view eastward and to the north was less interesting. It was mostly jungle, hills and ravines, briars, palm trees, and rough ground. And, as the Americans knew, many more enemy troops.

Lieutenant General Obata and the few remaining enemy officers were busy frantically trying to put together cohesive units with the intent to do all they could to slow the Americans' efforts to sweep the island. It would necessarily be a suicide endeavor. American victory was now inescapable. But the Japanese could and certainly would make it an even more costly one. That was now their mission, although the troops were assured they could and would shove the Americans back into the sea and celebrate a glorious victory.

After the heavy losses of Lieutenant General Takashina's counterattack, the defense of the higher ground of Mount Chachao, and the American assault ongoing on the Orote Peninsula, the surviving enemy troops used the lights of flares provided by the Americans during the night of July 28 to work their way along footpaths to the town of Ordot. That was near the middle of the island's narrowest point. From there, the troops were quickly organized into new companies and directed northeastward, where they were to quickly set up a line of blocking positions, ready to repel—or at least slow—the Marines as they inevitably moved in that direction.

Meanwhile, the American units were finding practically no resistance to the south and east of the two landing beaches. Reconnaissance patrols returned with reports of very few contacts. Just news that islanders were emerging from their homes and caves, enemy-run camps, or their own encampments they had dubbed "concentration camps," all to welcome their liberators with open arms and sobbing gratitude. The islanders seemed surprised to see American troops so soon after the invasion, but they were thrilled about it. Many were sick, malnourished, or simply dazed and dispirited from the constant mistreatment by the occupation forces of the IJA. While many had lost hope, they quickly recovered now that the Americans were back and the enemy on the run.

It was clear that the Japanese had chosen to move north-ward and dig in there to compel the invasion forces to take Guam back a foot at a time. And assure that process took as long and was as costly in terms of human life as possible.

While much of the terrain in more populated parts of the island ranged from flat to rolling, it was much less accommo-dating as the units headed north. Ravines cut deeply down hillsides and along the higher mountains. Rice paddies were numerous, especially on the flatter ground. The Japanese had forced islanders to create and manage paddies on just about ev-ery bit of low and relatively level ground on the island to pro-vide food for the troops. Now they served another purpose. They were difficult to cross on foot, in wheeled vehicles, and especially in tanks. The vegetation was thick, laced with bram-bles, and prevented advancing troops from seeing more than a few feet ahead. Landmarks were impossible to find, so it was easy to get lost and even end up in areas where other units were operating. It also made it very difficult to call in precise artil-lery strikes. Radioing the incorrect positions sometimes created losses by friendly fire.

Tanks found the going especially daunting. The deep ravines

virtually blocked their movement. Enemy tactics played off those obstacles. When the tanks used roadways—and they frequently had no other option—they encountered carefully planned roadblocks, antitank mines, and tank-killer guns. The enemy were well trained for facing the tanks and did not seem to fear them at all. Generally, when such an ambush was encountered, the tanks—at least those not incapacitated in the assault—backed off and waited, idling. Then artillery fire was requested. When the bombardment ended, the enemy that had survived the shelling backed away, only to set up another roadblock farther along the motorway.

The tank platoons quickly adapted some improvised procedures to improve their chances. Two Sherman M4A2 tanks would travel up a road, one on each side, bulldozing underbrush and clearing the way. Four infantrymen were assigned to each of those lead tanks, walking along closely behind, acting as eyes and ears, primarily watching for minefields or any signs of an ambush ahead. Meanwhile the rest of the group, usually three or four more tanks, followed the leading two by about a hundred yards. Field telephones were strapped to each tank's fender and the infantrymen used them to communicate with the crew inside the vehicle. The distinctive white stars on the sides of the tanks hand been painted over, since the Japanese tended to target them.

Two tanks were used to clear the way because they could lay down twice the fire in case of an attack, and if they were swarmed by ground troops, they were able to use their machine guns—typically .30-caliber weapons—to knock off each other the attackers who climbed aboard. This practice was dubbed "back-scratching."

The Shermans typically carried an M2 .50-caliber machine gun, but those were now often being removed. In other island invasions, enemy ground troops had managed to climb atop the tanks and turn their .50-calibers on the American ground troops who were following on foot. Even though the enemy soldiers employing such tactics had no cover and were soon killed, they still managed to take a toll on Marines.

As Lieutenant General Obata established his temporary command post at Ordot and began funneling his troops to the northern reaches of Guam, General Roy Geiger threw him something of a curveball. Geiger knew his men had been fighting hard for a week now, but instead of ordering an immediate full-bore push to the north, they would instead concentrate on eliminating any last elements of resisting Japanese in the area already assumed to be under their control. And also to get some rest as best they could in order to be fresh for the next push.

That push came on July 29, W-Day plus eight.

Obata was expecting the Marines to come rushing his way either that Wednesday night or early the next morning. He had counted his assets and come up with about 1,000 infantrymen, 800 naval rifle troops, and approximately 2,500 primarily support troops. Among the latter was Sergeant Shoichi Yokoi, although he had not acted in his usual capacity of supply sergeant in weeks. He now carried a rifle and a belt full of grenades. And he was still willing to fight on for the cause, hopeless as it might have looked by this time.

"We Japanese soldiers were told to prefer death to the disgrace of getting captured alive," he would later explain.

Lieutenant General Obata had taken stock and believed he had a few thousand more troops scattered about the island, but most of them north of a line from Sumay on the west to Pago Bay on the east coast, denoting a line that marked off about the northern two-thirds of Guam. He had only a half dozen artillery pieces left, but he did still have at his disposal two tank companies. As it turned out, those would come in very handy for the balance of the campaign. Their existence would actually preclude the Americans from officially declaring the island to be under their control.

When the Americans did not come charging his way, Obata took the opportunity to solidify his defensive plans. He would place his primary shielding lines from near Tumon Bay on the west coast, across the slimmest part of the island, to near Mount Barrigada, a 675-foot peak, and the tiny village of Barrigada, which had fewer than two dozen houses. The Finegayan–Barrigada Road would be a rough marker of the line. Once his troops were overrun—and the general knew quite well that was the reality of the situation—the survivors would retreat to the higher ground of Mount Barrigada, then do more delay-and-damage operations from there. Finally, a last stand would take place on 870-foot Mount Santa Rosa, a peak on the island's east coast overlooking the Pacific, about eight miles northeast of Barrigada. Many of his wounded troops had already been taken to the back side—the northeast slope—of Santa Rosa. When the time came, even those injured men—at least those who were conscious—would be given weapons and ordered to take as many of the invaders with them as they could.

The plan was identical to the one Obata had concocted for the defense of Saipan in the face of overwhelming numbers. It had worked well. There, the Japanese had prolonged the completion of the invasion for three weeks before launching a final suicidal counterattack designed to do nothing more than kill as many Americans as they possibly could while sacrificing themselves.

There were two big differences for Obata on Guam, however. The island was much wider than Saipan. And he had far fewer troops left with which to prolong the invasion. His defensive line would necessarily be much thinner, and each loss would diminish the effort far more.

On August 1, Obata moved his command post to near Mount Santa Rosa even as his mismatched array of troops dug in along the designated defensive line. Each man was aware that the next few days would produce a battle to the death. They knew they would not live to return home or see their families or enjoy the magnificent victory once the Empire inevitably prevailed.

Obata was feeling the pressure. In notes found later, he wrote, "The enemy air forces seeking our units during the daylight hours in the forest bombed and strafed even a single soldier." He also noted the intensity of the artillery, the naval gun bombardments, the attacking aircraft, and the continual presence of spotter planes droning overhead. He was aware, too, of the tanks rumbling in his direction and the overwhelming numbers of Marines and infantry that were steadily coming his way.

Still he pressed his men to harden their defenses and their resolve. It would be up to them to punish the invaders, and they would do so to the extent of their abilities.

General Geiger and his other commanders were certain the turning point of the assault on Guam had been reached. After raising the flag on Orote Peninsula, the next celebration would come when he could declare the island secure. One strong indication that this would not come easily was that practically no Japanese had surrendered. Few had even been captured, and those were almost always wounded and unable to resist. These men fought to the end or committed suicide rather than be captured. Only a handful had come running at the Americans with white flags tied to their rifle barrels.

According to captured enemy documents and the activity observed from aircraft, the Japanese had done as expected and continued to retreat northward. The jungle was denser and the terrain more imposing there.

On July 30, General Geiger sent units in pursuit of the retreating enemy troops, primarily along the west coast of the island. They found little opposition and were able to quickly secure Agaña. The recapture of the capital had symbolic as well as tactical value. Units of the 3rd Battalion, 3rd Marines, entered Agaña—or the ruins of Agaña—fully expecting enemy riflemen and snipers. They did encounter a few, most of whom were either stragglers or wounded men who had been handed rifles and told to deter the Americans. The centerpiece of the town and the island—the Plaza de España and the Catholic church—were declared secure after less than half an hour.

The formerly peaceful and lovely town of Agaña, like Sumay,

had been obliterated during the pre-invasion bombardment. That was because those planning the assault had not wanted to repeat the fierce house-to-house fighting experienced at the town of Garapan on Saipan a month earlier. Called "the Tokyo of the South Seas" by the Japanese, Garapan was virtually flattened during the American invasion, with an especially heavy loss of life among civilians there. It would not be repopulated until the late 1960s.

With both civilians and military standing at attention, a small American flag, one that had been made by hand and in secrecy by Guamanians during the Japanese occupation, was raised on the flagpole at the Plaza de España on July 30. Fittingly, it was within sight of where naval Governor George McMillin formally surrendered the island to the Japanese in December 1941.

Before darkness fell that night, roads leading to Finegayan and Barrigada were seized. That would help prepare for a charge against the well-fortified enemy positions that the Marines expected in those towns.

On the eastern side of the island, infantry troops had pushed all the way to the sea with little to no resistance. They set up a camp at Pago Bay near the town of Yona.

The next day, troops located a Japanese forced-labor camp at Asinan and freed about 2,000 grateful Guamanians. They received food and medical care and were allowed to return to their homes. That is, if they were still standing. Providing housing for the people of the island would be something of a problem, since fighting still raged, but many found refuge with friends and family.

The Marines would soon take control of the Agaña–Pago road, a hard-surface east–west route that gave the Americans a fine way to get back and forth across the island. Analysts would later determine this seemingly minor accomplishment was, in fact, a key to the ultimate success of the assault on Guam. Still, the road was poorly maintained, and because of the rain and the sudden excessive traffic it required attention. Even as the Marines mopped up a few enemy soldiers who had not been able to pull back, men and equipment from the Seabees were working on that and other vital roadways. Fortunately, most bridges remained intact, although some required a bit of shoring up.

The primary impediment to the eventual push northward was not enemy troops but the large numbers of mines and booby traps placed in the roadways and along stretches of flat ground. The occupiers knew such areas would most likely become a route for the movement of infantry, tanks, and artillery. The 25th Naval Construction Battalion and the engineers of the 19th Marines showed up to clear a safe path.

Despite these issues, a few of the units were moving so rapidly that it became a problem to resupply them. Their supply dumps were more than sixteen miles to the rear and there were no good roads to get the matériel to them. What few transportation routes that existed were not well maintained and the monsoon season rains had left them treacherous. Engineers did begin building an east–west roadway farther north of the Agaña–Pago road, but there were doubts it would be necessary if the quick assault continued at its current pace.

The Marines encountered their next stiff resistance on August 2 near the village of Barrigada. One of the primary objectives of the units approaching the town was to capture its water reservoir. Water was in short supply on Guam despite the daily drenching rainfall. A tank company had been sent out early in the morning and it quickly advanced beyond Barrigada to the vicinity of the tiny village of San Antonio. There, the tanks made contact with a sizable enemy force, General Obata's next line of defense.

The company immediately withdrew and reported the impressive number of defenders that they had encountered. This news, along with other action that morning, gave the Americans a rather good idea of where the Japanese had set up their defensive line. Sure enough, as the infantry made a push into the area, they met the strongest resistance they had seen in several days. They first engaged the enemy but then pulled back for the night. Measures were taken to protect their flank, getting ready for what could well be another screaming suicide charge in the dark of night.

None came. That meant the Marine assault on Barrigada would commence at first light on August 3, as planned.

Residents in the area confirmed that the enemy had been streaming through over the past two days, obviously regrouping, and then quickly falling back to set up a new defensive line. They also verified intelligence and observational reports that the line would be about a mile and a half beyond Barrigada, on the high ground of the slope up Mount Barrigada. That offered not only elevation but a thick jungle cover. From there, they would be able to hit advancing American troops coming through the open ground where the little town was located.

Sure enough, the fire from the shoulder of the mountain

was like a hailstorm. American tank fire and the booming distant artillery allowed a slow advance. It would require a full two days for the Marines to capture the town, its precious freshwater well, and, finally, the crest of Mount Barrigada.

Again, when it was inevitable that the American forces were going to overrun the Japanese positions, the Imperial Japanese Army troops melted into the jungle. From there they regrouped and set up another perimeter, from which they dared the invaders to attack.

Meanwhile, another point in the Japanese line of defense offered an even more difficult challenge to the rush northward. Those were the well-armed enemy positions at Finegayan and Yigo, two villages to the north and west of Barrigada. Each settlement stood as imposing barricades along the only roadway available to the Americans if they hoped to reach and clear Mount Santa Rosa.

That peak, Mount Santa Rosa, was now a primary goal. Everything pointed to the Japanese having decided to make a last-ditch stand there, to fight until the last man had died for the cause. And the longer they had to fortify their positions, the more difficult—and the more painful the cost in human life—the desperate battle would be.

Now, with a much clearer idea of the enemy's intentions and lines of defense—based on seized documents, captured troops, aerial reports, and the observations of the many Guamanians—a plan for the final stages of the battle was formulated. The Army's 77th Division, fresh off taking Barrigada and its shadowing mountain, were ordered to take out the enemy positions in Yigo and then move on to claim Mount Santa Rosa. The 3rd Marine

Division was to take on the Japanese at Finegayan and then race ahead to claim the remainder of the northern stretches of the island. Other units were still engaged in mopping up, removing pockets of trapped enemy soldiers all over Guam—many of whom lurked deeply in caves—as well as solidifying defenses, building shelters, roads, and airstrips, amassing equipment and supplies to support the ongoing invasion, and caring for the people of the island who had suffered so badly.

The family of Antonio Artero, still in their hideout in the ravine and cave on their ranch—the place where George Tweed had ridden out much of the occupation—had watched with mixed feelings the long air assault by the Americans, followed by the appearance of more and more ships on the horizon as the invasion had drawn near. The young girl, Carmen Artero, would later recall emerging from the cave to watch the American ships come tantalizingly close to the shoreline far below. Sometimes she jumped up and down, waved, and called to them, hoping they would come for her family. They never acknowledged the little girl.

The condition of Antonio's wife, Josefa, had worsened. The miscarriage and bleeding threatened to claim her life. Rescue by the Americans might be the only way to save her—if it was not too late already. Antonio also knew the devastating pre-assault barrage was leaving the island in shambles, that many of their friends and family had almost certainly died, and more would be lost as war raged across Guam. He also feared that the Japanese, now desperate, were likely to commit even worse atrocities than the chilling ones they were already hearing about.

Carmen remembers her father climbing down a sheer cliff to a pool of fresh water and bringing some back for her mom. The young girl was sick, too, running a fever, and she had to share the precious water with her mother. Food was running out and it was unsafe to go down the mountain to try to find any. Earlier in their stay in George Tweed's former lair, Carmen and her sister would occasionally make the long, hazardous trek down the trail to try to find eggs in the henhouse at the ranch. Once, they were stopped by a Japanese soldier. They told him where they were going, to get eggs from their chickens. He followed, stole the eggs, but did not question where the girls' parents might be. Now such an errand would be out of the question.

The family spent nights sitting in the darkness, saying the rosary, praying the Americans would soon come and liberate them. But one night, sick, hungry, and scared, young Carmen threw her rosary beads down the hillside. She was simply tired of praying. She had ultimately decided that God could no longer hear them anyway. Rescue by the *Americanos* seemed so near yet so far away. She feared none of her family would live to see it.

The Arteros were still wary when they finally heard voices one day from down below their hiding place. They had heard Japanese many times in the past weeks. This time, though, they did not sound like Japanese. One of the men was a cousin of theirs, who yelled to the Arteros that he was accompanied by American soldiers. Before her father went down the trail to meet the men, he told the cousin to request the soldiers remove their helmets so he could be sure they were *Americanos*. They obliged. Only then did Antonio Ortero come down to tell them about his sick wife and hungry children in the cave in the ravine.

Carmen recollects an abundance of crying and hugging, soldiers and family members alike. The troops led them down to a clearing. Along the way, she saw bodies of dead Japanese soldiers hanging in trees, tossed there by artillery shells and bombs. More enemy bodies were piled alongside the trail, and many were visible on the narrow beach at the foot of the cliffs where they had jumped to their deaths.

Finally, Josefa Artero was able to see a doctor. Then, as they ate and drank—the most food they had seen in weeks—Josefa suddenly broke into tears. She grabbed Carmen, hugging her closely to her.

"Your birthday! It is your birthday!" she said between sobs.

Indeed it was. This was the first time Carmen had even thought of it. There was another reason to celebrate the day the Americans rescued her and her family.

Antonio Palomo, still only a young boy of twelve, had seen much in the previous two years. He did not really understand what was happening with the Americans. He and his friends climbed trees on the hillsides overlooking the landing beaches and saw soldiers running ashore, and equipment following. Some vehicles were on fire out near the reef. He remembers thinking that these soldiers were not Japanese. They were taller and bigger. When the shooting and explosions let up, the children went down to greet the American Marines and beg for candy and chewing gum. The soldiers somehow managed to find some and shared it with them even as the troops tried to make certain Palomo and the other children stayed out of the line of fire.

Some of the islanders returned to their homes or farms if they were still there and habitable. Some began tending crops again, trying to raise food for their families and neighbors. Others moved into compounds where they would have shelter from the rains and receive food and medicine. One of the largest such compounds was at the Catholic cemetery in Anigua, just west of Agaña, where more than 7,000 Guamanian survivors were eventually placed. Dry campsites were provided amid the smashed tombstones. Within a few days the camp was full of activity, with chow lines and hastily built toilet facilities under the direction of the Marine Corps civil affairs team. Water was still in short supply. The island's freshwater system had been destroyed in the prelude to the invasion. At the survivors' camp, people carried whatever containers they could find and lined up for their daily ration of water from the Marine trailer. Even so, the worst of the ordeal was now over for them. The bulk of the rebuilding effort would begin as soon as the last Japanese had been killed or captured.

The night of August 2–3, the roads around Finegayan were ferociously hit with American artillery in preparation for the advance on that tiny village. As it turned out, the fusillade did little to daunt the Japanese defenders.

At 0700 on August 3—W-Day plus fourteen—the 3rd and 9th Marines pushed ahead, determined to shove the enemy out of their way and take this prime objective. Among them was PFC Frank Peter Witek, the BAR gunner and scout from the Chicago area. Just after 0900, the Americans ran squarely into a roadblock near the village. The Japanese were well hidden in the dense undergrowth overlooking a crossroads below them. The previous night's pummeling appeared to have had no effect on them. They had chosen a position that offered a clear view of the approaching Marines. It would take a massive effort by the tanks and the troops following them to finally move past the deadly block and take Finegayan, an otherwise unremarkable village in Guam's interior. One commander of units in the fight would later maintain this was the toughest opposition he had yet seen on Guam. More than seven hundred Japanese troops were eventually killed there.

PFC Witek was caught in the middle of the mayhem. His Medal of Honor citation would describe a soldier who demonstrated unbelievable bravery in attacking the enemy but also an inspiring willingness to risk his own life to help wounded fellow Marines during the fight for the key crossroads:

"When his rifle platoon was halted by heavy surprise fire from well camouflaged enemy positions, Private First Class Witek daringly remained standing to fire a full magazine from his automatic [rifle] point-blank range into a depression housing Japanese troops, killing eight of the enemy and enabling the greater part of his platoon to take cover. During his platoon's withdrawal for consolidation of lines, he remained to safeguard a severely wounded comrade, courageously returning the enemy's fire until the arrival of stretcher bearers and then covering the evacuation by sustained fire as he moved backward toward his own lines. With his platoon again pinned down by a hostile machine gun, Private First Class Witek, on his own initiative, moved forward boldly ahead of the reinforcing tanks and infantry, alternately throwing hand grenades and firing as he advanced to within five to ten yards of the enemy position, destroying the hostile machine-gun emplacement and an additional eight Japanese before he, himself, was struck down by an enemy rifleman. His valiant and inspiring action effectively reduced the enemy's firepower, thereby enabling his platoon to attain its objective, and reflects the highest credit upon Private First Class Witek and the United States Naval Service. He gallantly gave his life for his country."

When his Marine buddies recovered Witek's body, they discovered that he only had eight cartridges left out of the original 240 rounds he had been issued. He would be buried in the Marine Corps Cemetery on Guam, but later, after the war, his body was exhumed and reinterred at the Rock Island National Cemetery in Rock Island, Illinois. As was the case with his fellow Marine PFC Leonard Mason, Frank Witek would receive the Medal of Honor posthumously.

Even when the Marines were certain they had secured the village of Finegayan, they were suddenly surprised by two enemy tanks that appeared in the undergrowth at a nearby junction. The tanks shot up the area and, despite counterfire, got away up the road toward Mount Santa Rosa.

Then, just as unexpectedly, mortar rounds began exploding among the Marines, obviously as cover for another half dozen or so enemy tanks that broke from the underbrush and raced at the Americans. They, too, did their best to kill as many men as they could before wheeling around and hightailing it just as artillery shells started raining down on them. They were gone before the Marines could even chase after them or redirect the artillery onslaught. It was clear the Japanese only intended to unleash as much carnage as they could before the Americans had the opportunity to fight back or call in help, demonstrating to the invaders that they still had perfectly serviceable and deadly tanks and that they would use them to stop or slow down the U.S. forces.

After the brutal battle for Finegayan, the plan was for the 3rd Marine Division to move northward, eventually taking Ritidian Point. That was the island's northernmost tip and the spot where the very first invaders—Saipan natives and not yet the Japanese—had come ashore two and a half years earlier. But the artillery barrage of the night before and the battle for the town had not dented the enemy opposition in the area. Reconnaissance patrols ran into strong resistance along the road and the few trails through the jungle north of Finegayan. After some spirited fighting, although they inflicted some harm on the Japanese, the patrols pulled back and rethought the plan to hurry to Ritidian.

Nothing came easy. General Geiger and his staff had known from the beginning that the Japanese would continue to obstruct the Marine advance in whatever manner necessary, countering any move to claim more of the north part of Guam. And they were now sure Mount Santa Rosa, almost seven miles north of the hard-won village of Barrigada, would be well defended and prepared to stall the takeover of the island. The mountain also presented yet another location with impossibly rough terrain, with steep slopes crisscrossed by rugged gullies and blanketed by almost impenetrable tropical forest. Tank unit commanders were already reporting their tanks passing within fifteen feet without even being aware of one another's presence. Also, once again, the enemy had the elevation on their side, and just enough open ground that snipers and machine guns could rake the gaps in the foliage, with deadly results.

As August 6 dawned, and as long-gestating plans were crystallized for the capture of Mount Santa Rosa and the run to Ritidian Point, the liberators were still reluctant to make predictions for their higher-ups. Even with the intelligence they had, they simply did not know how many enemy troops were still out there, where they were, or how much longer it would be before they would have complete control of Guam. And when the largest island in the Marianas would be in Allied hands.

An even bigger question was just how many men would have to die—on both sides—before that goal would finally be realized.

CHAPTER ELEVEN

GHOST SOLDIERS

The first U.S. bombs fell on Guam on June 11, 1944. Shells were launched from Navy vessels offshore about the same time. The attacks had continued almost daily for most of a month and a half, first as "softening up" for the planned invasion, then in support of ground troops trying to clear the island of enemy troops. Much of the tropical landscape now looked as if it had been bulldozed and set afire. Island residents were seriously shell-shocked but still hopeful the fighting on their war-ravaged island home was about to end.

The Marine and Army units had thrown their best punches. Progress had varied from too fast for replenishment and support to maddeningly and frustratingly slow. But the end was finally in sight.

On August 7—W-Day plus seventeen—the bulk of the relentless Japanese resistance had been cornered in the northern third of Guam and mostly around the peak of Mount Santa Rosa, overlooking the sea from the island's east coast. Still, General Roy Geiger and his command staff had big questions. Just how many enemy troops were still out there? He knew only approximately how many were dead or captured. And the previous estimates of pre-assault enemy strength. Simple arithmetic indicated an intimidating number of Japanese unaccounted for, soldiers who had possibly managed to survive.

Indeed, island residents confirmed having seen large numbers of enemy constantly filtering northward after abandoning temporary lines of defense. Some compared them to ghosts, barely visible, moving quietly at night in the dark jungle mist. And they still had those pesky tank units and a proven way of deploying them to effect the most damage to pursuing ground troops.

The big quandary: How would the enemy commanders use those remaining troops? Would they stage a suicidal attack as they had done on Saipan? Or would they dig in and fight a delaying battle until every single Imperial Japanese Army soldier or officer was dead or apprehended? The invasion force leaders would have to prepare for both possibilities.

The Americans were now using night fighters, so the Japanese no longer operated unchallenged in the tropical darkness. Now that the enemy defensive lines had been broken, the night patrols had been able to eliminate many pockets of stragglers, who tended to work through the night, constructing and manning machine-gun nests or sniper positions and awaiting the

Americans when they began moving with first daylight. Nocturnal patrols put a damper on those tactics.

Even though heavy and costly fighting had been going on for almost three weeks, some units had been able to get rest and recuperate. One of those was the U.S. Army's 306th Infantry Regiment, which had been patrolling the southern part of the island, rarely engaging with stragglers, mostly helping Guamanians get settled in again. Now the regiment moved north to join the battle-weary 9th Marines with orders to proceed up the road to Yigo, take that village, then prepare for the assault on Santa Rosa. They would circle around and come at the peak from the west and north in a pincer assault with forces from the south, all preceded by air and artillery attacks.

If anyone believed the way to Santa Rosa would be easy, an incident on August 6 illustrates just how deadly and difficult it would be. Colonel Douglas McNair, a highly respected officer, was the chief of staff of the Army's 77th Infantry Division. He and two others—an enlisted man and another officer—were diligently searching for the best location for a division command post to support the upcoming assault. His citation for the posthumous awarding of the Silver Star says, "Colonel McNair encountered three Japanese soldiers in a native hut about three hundred yards from the main road. Cautiously approaching the entrance to the hut, Colonel McNair fired several times and directed the movements and fire of his companion(s). The Japanese in the hut returned the fire and during the exchange Colonel McNair was struck and killed. Colonel McNair's gallantry, courage and aggressive and unhesitating leadership was an inspiration to his companions and to the entire Division."

Colonel McNair's boss, Major General A. D. Bruce, commanding general, 77th Infantry Division, was even more emphatic about what kind of man was shot down outside the simple native hut that day:

"In two wars I have seen many men who had courage, who worked until they were about to drop, who were professionally efficient, who knew how to handle troops, who had a sense of humor, but Doug had more than these qualifications. He had intellectual honesty and courage of his convictions far above the average. He not only was brave in the face of danger but was morally brave. He was unusual in his lack of selfishness in order to promote the common good of the Division. Our Division and our country lost a great soldier."

But there are other sad aspects to the story of this one man's loss among so many. Not only did he leave a widow and a daughter, Bonnie Claire, who was not yet a year old, but Colonel McNair had lost his own father, another well-respected and honored military man, only twelve days before his own death.

Like his son, a West Point graduate, Lieutenant General Lesley J. McNair was a career soldier who saw action in both world wars. He was killed by friendly fire during action in France, where he was commander of a group that did not even exist. The fictitious "First United States Army Group" was part of "Operation Quicksilver," an elaborate deception to distract the Germans from the actual invasion of Normandy on D-Day. An Eighth Air Force bomb fell into his foxhole as the Army provided close air support of infantry operations as part of the Battle of Normandy.

As far as we know, the younger McNair had not yet heard of

the death of his father half a world away when he lost his own life on the road to Yigo on Guam.

The assault on Mount Santa Rosa started at high noon on August 7. There was the typical pounding of artillery accompanied by the rumble of tanks, followed closely by ground troops. Bulldozers accompanied the tanks, cutting trails through the jungle as best they could. Machine-gun nests were overrun beneath the treads of the tanks and dozers, then annihilated by troops with dynamite and flamethrowers. Aerial bombardment had already commenced, concentrated on Yigo and what few emplacements the pilots could see on the mountain itself.

The village was taken quickly as the enemy characteristically vanished into the jungle. By late afternoon the American troops began setting up for the night, aware the Japanese could suddenly emerge screaming from the thick jungle, seeking to break through the line.

But again the anticipated counterattack failed to materialize.

Early the next day, two American regiments were on the move. By just after noon, and after some heavy going, they reported that they had reached and secured the north half of Mount Santa Rosa. They did not intend to stop there. Indeed, by mid-afternoon, the Army units—the 305th and 307th Regiments—had fought their way to the high cliffs on the peak's east side and could peer down into the blue waters of the Pacific Ocean. And also see bodies of Japanese troops who had apparently jumped to their deaths.

But the math still did not add up. From August 6 until dark on August 7, what was expected to be a heavily defended enemy command post at Yigo had been quickly taken. And the assumed location of the final stand by the Japanese on Mount Santa Rosa was already in American hands. Fighting had been fierce in spots, but it had mostly been small units dug in, fighting to the death as the superior American forces rolled over them. Yet there were only about six hundred bodies to show for the effort.

Best estimates were that 5,000 troops remained. And there were several enemy tank units that had not yet been taken out or even spotted during the clashes.

There was only one conclusion: thousands of enemy soldiers were hiding all over the island and would have to be ferreted out one or two at a time. And each one of them had solemnly sworn to die for the emperor. Guam was infested with thousands of deadly rattlesnakes gone to ground.

One key objective remained: locating and taking out the Imperial Japanese Army's commanding officer and what remained of his staff. Movement on one hill north of Santa Rosa indicated that this might well be where General Obata had set up yet another temporary command post.

As Marines and Army mopped up the area they had so hastily run through on the way to Santa Rosa, they spotted still more Japanese who had committed ritual suicide rather than surrender and become prisoners of war. At other points, enemy soldiers charged madly from cover, intent on killing Americans before they were struck down. And a group from the 21st Marines made a grisly discovery as they moved up a roadway toward Ritidian Point. They happened upon the bodies of thirty Chamorros, every one of them beheaded, and the massacre had obviously occurred recently.

The 1st Provisional Marine Brigade reached Ritidian Point on August 8. That gave the unit a signal distinction. They had been the first to reach the southernmost point on Guam early in the battle and had now become the first group to arrive at the northernmost spot.

The latter had not been easy, though. And it was not necessarily because of the enemy. Resistance had been minimal. P-47 aircraft from the Seventh Air Force base on Saipan had conducted their last bombing and strafing runs on the point, and that had apparently been enough to chase the enemy into the ground. But the narrow, hazardous trail along the face of a cliff that led them to Ritidian had been a frightening hike for the Marines.

From the tops of the cliffs, they could now look down to the beach far below and see fellow Marines clearing numerous caves.

At 1800 hours on August 9, the Marine commander in the zone declared there was no more organized enemy resistance in his area.

There certainly had been the night before. That was when the 3rd Marines found out where the Japanese tank units had gone. It was near the little town of Tarague, on the northeast corner of the island. Marines had been clearing the area of stragglers and a few machine-gun nests when mortar rounds landed all around them. Then the unmistakable metallic clattering of tank treads emerging from impossibly thick jungle. And all in the middle of a downpour.

Bazooka rockets and antitank grenades were soaked by the rain and did not work. The enemy attacked viciously, launching rounds into the Marine positions before finally pulling back and disappearing into the brush.

The unit's commander expected the worst outcome as he assayed his losses. But, miraculously, there was not a single man hurt or killed.

Also on August 8, the 9th Marines reached Pati Point on the northeast coastline. There had been reports of as many as 2,000 enemy troops hiding in the thick vegetation there. The decision was made not to stage an attack on them—not this late in the operation. The enemy soldiers were virtually trapped with the sea on three sides and the Americans behind them. Instead, a massive artillery attack was ordered. Some Marines later reported it was the most impressive shelling display they had ever witnessed. More than 2,000 rounds thundered down on the small area of jungle and tall grass.

When it was over, the Marines found evidence of many enemy troops killed, though certainly not 2,000. Survivors were either taken prisoner or shot when they resisted.

With opposition minimal, there was the temptation to declare Guam secure. But it decidedly was not. In addition to there still being thousands of enemy troops unaccounted for, there was also the issue of the tank units that had made their appearance on August 8 near Tarague. General Geiger assumed they could continue looking for the troops hiding in caves and the jungle, and likely would be doing so for months to come.

But there was a very good reason for urgency in eliminating those missing tanks as soon as they could.

Admiral Chester Nimitz, the big boss of the Navy in this

part of the war, was coming for a visit on the tenth. The enemy tanks would, without question, have to be eliminated by then.

Second Battalion, 3rd Marines, drew the assignment. Early on the morning of August 10, the battalion, accompanied by a platoon of Sherman tanks of their own, came across two Japanese medium tanks. The enemy tanks opened fire and the battle was on. It did not take the Shermans long to wipe out the challengers, leaving them smoking, dead. Then they found seven more medium tanks abandoned in the jungle a short distance behind. They had run out of fuel before they were able to engage the Americans.

The Marines took off after the enemy tank crews and soon found them. Along with an infantry platoon, the Japanese had decided to make a stand, fighting with their backs to the coastal cliffs. From that untenable position, the Marines made quick work of wiping them out.

A report of the successful attack and the destruction of what appeared to be the enemy's last tanks got to General Geiger at 1130 on August 10. Without hesitation, he made the declaration that all organized resistance on Guam had come to an end.

Just in time for the visit by Admiral Nimitz.

Even happier about the declaration were the long-suffering Guamanians. Their anguish was not yet over. Their beautiful island had been demolished by years of brutal war. Neighbors, friends, and family had died. Roadways and other infrastructure had been demolished. Farmland was cratered by bombs and shells. Homes were now rubble. But finally they could see the end.

And they were once again a proud part of the United States of America. They assumed the United States would certainly be dedicated to helping them all get back on their feet.

In addition to the ghostly thousands of enemy troops still out there somewhere, there was one other hanging thread. Lieutenant General Hideyoshi Obata, the overall commander of Japanese forces in Palau, the Marianas, the Marshall Islands, the Carolines, the Bonins, and the Volcano Islands, the man who had been unexpectedly forced to ride out the battle for the Mariana Islands on Guam—the commander who was required to take direct charge of Guam's defense when the island's commander was killed early in the struggle—was apparently still out there somewhere. While not necessary to declare victory on the last of the Marianas, capturing or killing the general would tie a nice ribbon around the effort.

Unbeknownst to the Americans, Obata had ultimately retreated to Mount Mataguac, west of Mount Santa Rosa and the village of Yigo. There he was bound to ride out whatever might happen. There was simply no place for him to go except into the sea.

In anticipation of an American invasion, the Japanese had built two sturdy concrete bunkers on Mount Mataguac. They had been constructed in a deep ravine just down from the 630-foot summit. There they would have access to fresh water. They would also be well hidden from both aircraft and approaching troops by the dense bamboo that grew all around them. It was an almost perfect position from which to protect the island's military commander and his few remaining staff members.

Although they had no idea who was inside the bunker, elements of the 306th Regiment of the 77th Infantry Division of the U.S. Army located and attacked the installation early on the morning of August 11. They persisted despite especially strong resistance. There was clearly some reason why the defense of the bunkers was so intense.

Just before the attack, General Obata managed to get one last message to the commanders of the Imperial Japanese Army and to his emperor back in Japan: "We are continuing a desperate battle. We have only our bare hands to fight with. The holding of Guam has become hopeless. Our souls will defend the island to the very end. I am overwhelmed with sorrow for the families of the many officers and men. I pray for the prosperity of the Empire."

Shortly after, the U.S. Army troops threw everything they had at the bunkers. After fighting it out with the enemy troops guarding the installation—seven U.S. soldiers died and seventeen were wounded on the day after Guam was declared to be "secure"—the Americans used white-phosphorous grenades, pole charges, and more than four hundred blocks of TNT to destroy everything in sight. The entrances to the bunkers were sealed solidly.

It would be three days later before engineers used bulldozers to open them up again. They found sixty Japanese bodies inside. One of them was that of Lieutenant General Hideyoshi Obata.

There was no way to determine if Obata had committed suicide or if he had died in the fierce, fiery attack on his and

Japan's final formal refuge on Great Shrine Island. Those who found his body were convinced it was the former. Obata was fifty-four years old at the time of his death.

Later in the war, the Imperial Japanese Army promoted him posthumously to the rank of full general.

★ CHAPTER TWELVE ★

YOKOI'S CAVE

With the pronouncement that the Second Battle of Guam was officially over, Major General Henry L. Larsen assumed the Guam Island Command at noon on August 15, 1944. One of his staff's major objectives was to tabulate losses on both sides during the struggle. Roughly 1,800 Americans had been killed in action or by accidental injury and just over 7,000 wounded. About 700 Chamorros died during the occupation, mostly executed by the Japanese, and untold more were murdered by the enemy during the liberation by the Americans.

The official tally of enemy dead was 10,971 men, based on actual bodies counted. Another 485 had been captured. That confirmed once again that about 10,000 Japanese soldiers and sailors were still on the island somewhere, dead or alive. None could have escaped.

From experience, the American forces also knew any who were still alive had taken a solemn oath to fight to the death in support of the emperor and the Empire of Japan. For sure, some of them staged ambushes, alone or in small groups. Others sniped at the Americans until their ammunition ran out. After a few weeks—and with no small irony—most of them became foragers, seeking food. Some were captured attempting to break into buildings at night where stores were kept. Others were shot before they had opportunity to shoot first. Guamanians were plagued by desperately hungry Japanese soldiers breaking into their homes, looking for food. But the natives, most of whom were now armed, either shot them or captured them and turned them over to the Marines.

As the mop-up continued, more bodies were found, most of whom appeared to have succumbed to hunger, dysentery, previously inflicted wounds, or other disease. Some had obviously used a last bullet or grenade to commit suicide or had leapt off one of the island's tall cliffs onto the rocky beaches below.

Early in the process, American patrols were crisscrossing the passable parts of the island, capturing or killing almost a hundred Japanese stragglers a day. They could only guess how many more hid in the jungles, ravines, and caves, out of reach of the patrols, but with little hope for survival. Unlike Navy radioman George Tweed, they could not count on help from the Chamorros.

The remaining elusive Japanese were still dangerous. Almost five months after the formal end to hostilities on Guam,

Marine PFC Luther Woodward spotted a fresh footprint near an ammunition dump and knew immediately that it had been made by a Japanese soldier. Woodward, a member of one of the all–African American units—African Americans were not allowed to become Marines until 1942—would later receive a Silver Star for what he did that day. His citation says:

"Following a freshly made foot print which he had discovered in the vicinity of the ammunition dump, Private Woodard, voluntarily and unaided, trailed a party of six Japanese through heavy underbrush to a small clearing near an abandoned shack where he opened fire against the enemy killing one and possibly wounding another before the survivors fled. Returning to his company, Private Woodard organized a patrol of five men and when contact was again established with the hostile group was successful in killing one of the two who were annihilated by his group. His initiative and cool courage in the face of grave peril were in keeping with the highest traditions of the United States Naval Service."

The other five men Private Woodward organized into a patrol were also black Marines.

On April Fool's Day 1945, Sergeant Ezra Kelly, yet another one of the African American Marines, killed one of two Japanese stragglers whom he discovered within a thousand yards of the location where his unit was camped. Over the rest of the month, he and his buddies killed two more Japanese. During the rest of the summer, Kelly added to his tally, taking out a total of six Japanese who had been holding out on Guam.

Many of the troops viewed hunting down the hiding enemy soldiers as being good for morale. With fighting raging on other islands in the Pacific, men still based on Guam, and especially the black Marines, had been relegated to relatively mundane duty. By being a part of the search patrols, they felt they were a bigger part of the war, contributing to its successful end.

In all, during the time between the conclusion of the battle for Guam and the end of the war a year later, more than 8,500 additional Japanese troops were killed, captured, or found dead at various places around the island. But, as they were soon to learn, the Americans had still not eliminated all the enemy soldiers left there. On December 8, 1945, almost four months after the end of World War II, three Marines were ambushed and killed by one of those remaining enemy soldiers.

As with many of his fellow Imperial Japanese Army troops, Sergeant Shoichi Yokoi had done all he could to honor his promise to battle to the death to defend the island. During the final days of fighting, the American troops ripped through the lines he and his comrades had established, and despite the best effort of the Japanese troops, the Americans just kept coming. Amid the confusion, Yokoi became separated from the bulk of the defenders. Along with nine other IJA soldiers, he followed the path of least resistance and used barely visible trails to move south, negotiating the jungle and avoiding the invading troops. The goal was to find a hiding place. From there they could continue to do what they had been ordered to do: Delay the invasion forces. Disrupt the occupation. Create chaos. Kill as many Americans as possible and do it any way they could.

Yokoi and the others happened upon hiding places near

Talofofo, a village on a bay of the same name on Guam's remote southeastern coast. It is unknown if they were familiar with the area beforehand or discovered it while looking for cover. While the caves and ravines they hid in were often crowded for ten men, the accommodations would have to do. From there, they would continue their war on the Americans on behalf of the emperor. Even with practically no weapons. Or no ammunition for the weapons they did have.

They were quite surprised that they were not seeing many invaders in this area of the island. Most likely, the Americans were concentrating on the main body of IJA troops who were defending the north quadrant of Guam. Yokoi and his nine friends started their new existence by taking care of necessities: hunting for animals; raiding the gardens, chicken coops, and pig pens of islanders; searching for coconuts and other naturally growing native foods; finding a source for fresh water; and securing their cave, making certain it was well hidden.

Yokoi could have had no idea just how long he would eventually occupy that simple hole in a hillside near Talofofo.

As expected, the heavy cruiser USS *Indianapolis* (CA-35) steamed into Apra Harbor on August 10, 1944, with Admiral Chester Nimitz aboard. Accompanying the admiral was the commandant of the Marine Corps, General Alexander Vandegrift, just appointed to that position in January. Vandegrift, nicknamed "Sunny Jim," had also received the Medal of Honor personally from President Franklin Roosevelt at the White House the previous year for action in the Solomon Islands and specifically the assault on the island of Guadalcanal.

Both men were pleased with the news that organized hostilities had concluded. Even though the retaking of Guam had occurred almost two months later than originally planned, they were now ready to make good use of the reclaimed island. Admiral Nimitz announced that he would establish on Guam his forward headquarters as commander in chief, U.S. Pacific Fleet, and commander in chief, Pacific Ocean Areas. That meant he would oversee the rest of the war in the Pacific theater from the little island that had once been expendable, not worthy of defense.

The war in the Pacific was still far from over. Brutal battles on islands most Americans had never heard of before—but that would become well-known because of what U.S. troops would do there—were yet to come. Epic and bloody battles on Peleliu, Iwo Jima, the Philippines, and Okinawa.

Over the next few months, B-29 Superfortress bombers and other aircraft began lifting off from rebuilt and newly constructed airfields on Guam, as well as on Saipan and Tinian. From there, they inflicted severe damage on the Japanese Home Islands. No location was safe from the American bombs. Tinian, which had been captured by the United States only ten days before Guam was secured, quickly became the largest air base in the world, although the total land area of the island was only about forty square miles.

And a year later, in August 1945, it would be from Runway Able, North Field, on nearby Tinian that a B-29 called the *Enola Gay* for the pilot's mother would depart, carrying an atomic bomb bound for Hiroshima. Then, three days later, another plane would take off from Runway Able on Tinian, with an A-bomb that would be dropped on Nagasaki.

But lost in the historic magnitude of those two flights from the Mariana Islands is the fact that hundreds of conventional bombing runs were made from Guam, Saipan, and Tinian, both before and after "Little Boy" and "Fat Man," the two atomic bombs, fell on Japan. At one point during the final year of World War II, those three islands in the Marianas were home to more than 1,000 B-29 Superfortress bombers. Many historians still speculate that finally having the ability to fly the big bombers from the Marianas and inflict unbelievable damage on the Japanese Empire would have eventually brought the war with Japan to a close without using the A-bombs. Or without having to complete the planned invasion of the Home Islands.

That we will never know. But Guam, which had been left defenseless and was so quickly surrendered on the first day of World War II, had now become a key cog in America's Pacific war machine.

★ CHAPTER THIRTEEN ★

THE SPIRIT OF THE CHAMORROS

Admiral Chester Nimitz made it a point to send the people of Guam a personal message when World War II came to a formal conclusion on September 2, 1945. He was one of the signees of the peace accords on the deck of the battleship USS *Missouri* (BB-63) that day in Tokyo Bay. It was a photo of the admiral sitting at the small desk, putting his signature on the document that finally brought the bloody conflict—an especially horrendous one for native islanders on Guam—to an end. Beneath the photo—which also shows General Douglas MacArthur, Admiral William "Bull" Halsey Jr., and Admiral Raymond Spruance looking over his shoulder—Nimitz placed a handwritten inscription that says, "With best wishes and great admiration for the citizens of Guam who helped make possible the above peace."

They had indeed.

Two Chamorro sailors in the U.S. Navy, Ramon White and Frank B. Manibusan, both members of the admiral's staff, were present that day and witnessed the event aboard the *Missouri*.

Then there was Tony Duenas, the only Guam native to win the Silver Star for his service during the war. He was a deputized guide and scout for the Marines during the successful but costly assault on Guam.

And U.S. Navy yeoman Juan Santos Aflague, who was not on his home island when the war started. Instead, he was aboard a ship at Mindanao when the Japanese attacked the Philippines on December 8, 1941. His vessel managed to escape during the assault and joined the Asiatic fleet. It would be three long years before he would be able to return to Guam. Three years in which he was able to learn little of the fate of his family or the island on which he had grown up. He ultimately learned that his mother, brother, and brother-in-law had been killed during the Japanese occupation. But Major General Henry Larsen, after he assumed command of Guam, managed to get word to Yeoman Aflague that his wife and children were okay, safe, and well after the United States had taken back the island. When Aflague finally stepped ashore on Guam, he did not recognize the place. He even had difficulty locating his house. But it was still standing. His youngest son had no memory of his dad, who had left to serve his country when the boy was a baby.

The Marines and soldiers were very conscious of how grateful the Chamorros were for having liberated their island after the harsh occupation. Marine corporal Maury T. Williams Jr.

was a reconnaissance scout for the 21st Marines from Memphis, Tennessee. He and others from his unit were guarding positions just after clearing the last of the enemy from Agaña when they began noticing Chamorros emerging from the smoke and darkness and thick jungle.

"They were understandably quite emotional as they approached, considering their months of oppression under the Japanese, and nearly all had tears streaming down their faces," Williams later recalled. "Many were on foot but some of them came in the backs of trucks that had been dispatched to a pickup point a short distance ahead.

"But one large group, being brought through the lines in the back end of a six-by-six truck, were singing a song that must have been composed during the occupation. Their words expressed their love of America and Americans, including a line that said something like, 'Thank you, Uncle Sam.' Those folks weren't the only ones with tears streaming down their cheeks that day."

Indeed, there was unanimous joy and celebration, some for the liberation, some because things might finally get back to normal. When the Japanese first occupied Guam, Jesus Pangelinan decided there was no way he would allow his life savings to fall into their hands. He had already heard that he would be required to exchange his American dollars for greatly devalued Japanese yen. So he decided to bury his U.S. currency in a metal box in his backyard. And hope no bomb or Japanese invader found it. When liberation day finally came, Pangelinan searched the yard until he found the box and removed it from the muddy ground. The box was rusty after being buried for more than two years but it appeared to be intact. Sure enough, the dollars were still there, representing almost everything the family had. Their home had long since been destroyed, but they still had their life savings. And, thankfully, their lives.

A part of the 22nd Marines, Wesley T. Bush's unit had just been relieved and were in the process of moving back to a more secure area for some rest. This would be his first opportunity to interact with the people he and his fellow Marines had been fighting so hard to liberate. Though he was bone tired, he could not help but notice the exuberant spirit of the people he met.

"We had battled continuously for fourteen days, then got a rest," Bush later related. "As we marched to the rear, we went through an area where the lovely people of Guam had been gathered. The youngsters ran alongside of us holding on to our rifles. Old men held our hands and the women cried and cheered and patted our backs. All the hardship and misery and wounds we had suffered melted away at that moment and I said to myself, 'It has been worth it all.' I will never forget how grateful the people were."

Shortly after the Americans came ashore, and in the middle of a monsoon downpour, fifteen-year-old Jesus Lizama was asked to run an errand for his father. He was taking a basket of shrimp to trade with the Japanese for salt. Jesus was chosen for the chore because he was the only one in the group of forty Chamorros hiding in the jungle who spoke fluent Japanese. Suddenly, as he made his way through tall, dense grass, he found himself surrounded by U.S. Marines. The boy dropped the shrimp and put his hands in the air.

Once the Americans determined Lizama was not Japanese,

and as soon as they learned that he was part of a bunch of is-landers hiding out from the enemy, everyone relaxed. They sent two soldiers to where the other Chamorros were located to evacuate them to a place of relative safety. Then they asked the boy if he could guide them to a place they had been told about called Manengon. He agreed. When they got there, they chased away four Japanese guards who were overseeing a large group of Chamorros being held under brutal conditions in a prison camp. The American soldiers told them to stay low until they could be sure there were no more enemy close by. They were so excited to see the Americans, they refused to obey and began to dance and sing.

Another Guamanian who inadvertently became a civilian guide for the Americans was nineteen-year-old Jesse Perez. He had been forced to carry food supplies and ammunition for a platoon of ten Japanese soldiers. While on the way to Yigo as part of establishing defensive lines in the northern part of Guam, the soldiers stopped at a crossroads for a quick rest. Perez spotted an American soldier about fifty yards up the road, but the Japanese had not seen him.

Perez was able to sneak away from the Japanese and join what turned out to be a sizable American patrol. With the in-formation Perez shared with the patrol, they were able to am-bush and wipe out the Japanese platoon. The young man then became a guide for the Americans from then until he was wounded in a fierce fight near Yigo, his hometown. He ended up with a bullet lodged between two ribs that he would carry in his body for the rest of his life.

It was not unusual at all for Chamorros to become volunteer

scouts for the American invasion forces. Without their detailed knowledge of the island's geography, it would have been much more difficult to accomplish the mission of securing the island. Maps of most areas of the island were inadequate, because the thick jungle had kept aerial reconnaissance from seeing important details in the rough terrain. And because of their patriotism and the way the occupation forces had treated them and their families for the previous thirty-one months, the Chamorros were very motivated to help.

As a thirteen-year-old boy, Vicente "Ben" Blaz was forced by the Japanese to work in the rice paddies from daylight until dark each day. He would later write, "The Chamorro spirit was not an abstraction; rather, it was demonstrably real during those years and I have drawn inspiration and sustenance from that reality my entire life." After receiving a scholarship to the University of Notre Dame, Blaz went on to become a brigadier general in the U.S. Marine Corps and was later elected as a delegate to the U.S. House of Representatives from Guam from 1985 to 1993.

Blaz remembered sitting on logs around a campfire at night as their parents shared experiences and thoughts, just as generations of Chamorros had done. How, after a long day of forced labor, the men sang folk songs. He recalled how farmers joined together during the occupation to clear jungle so they could plant food to feed their families while the women cared for the sick, worked the gardens, and cooked over open fires.

General Blaz also wrote of a young Japanese officer he got to know who taught him a bit of the language in exchange for Blaz's father teaching the soldier English. One day the soldier innocently asked Blaz and his father why they were at war with each other. The Japanese officer had no idea what he was fighting for.

The soldier stopped by to tell the family goodbye as he went to help defend Guam from the U.S. assault. They would never know if he survived or died for what was, to him at least, an unknown cause.

But Blaz remembered most vividly "the joyous faces of my fellow Chamorros . . . who had endured thirty-one months of harsh enemy occupation, including internment in concentration camps, in a war they had no part in starting."

As a member of Congress, Blaz twice introduced a bill to make Guam a commonwealth, giving the islanders full citizenship, and other measures seeking the return by the United States of excess lands on the island and payment of war reparations. None of them were adopted.

Blaz later sadly stated, "We are equal in war, but not in peace."

Once the island was secure, the process of collecting intelligence that might be of help in other upcoming battles began almost immediately. Another Chamorro played a key and critical role in that effort. Adolfo Sgambelluri was a police officer and did work for U.S. Naval Intelligence before the Japanese invasion. He was detained by the invaders, but someone convinced the Japanese that he was Italian, not American or Guamanian, so he was set free. Because of his police detective background—he later claimed he learned to be an investigator by reading pulp detective magazines—the enemy forces put him in charge of stopping livestock "thefts" by the islanders, even though those islanders actually owned the animals and were merely trying to get their property back. He also served as a liaison between the Japanese and the island natives. Sgambelluri became a "double agent," helping his people while pretending to assist the Japanese, warning them of impending searches or crackdowns. He also played a key role in helping hide and protect George Tweed during his long ordeal avoiding capture by the invaders.

After the liberation, Sgambelluri volunteered to assist the Marines any way he could. He requested that he be put into a stockade with Japanese prisoners of war. There, he was to be treated as just another POW. Sgambelluri had risked his life many times during the Japanese occupation to try to help his people survive. This was nothing new to him. The Japanese prisoners only knew of his work during the occupation and assumed the Americans had imprisoned him for aiding the enemy. Had they known the real story, he would have been killed.

He would still pay a heavy price. For many years, he was accused of being a Japanese sympathizer by those who knew only of his work for the enemy during the occupation. That only intensified when the Americans threw him into the stockade with other POWs. But the information he was able to gather led to justice being meted out during the War Crimes Tribunal that was convened after the war.

Sgambelluri would ultimately be honored for his clandestine efforts. A letter from a U.S. Army colonel said, in part, "You performed your work in the highest of police tradition and I hope that all people now understand why you were in the stockade. It was a secret mission to make possible the trial of offenders against the Guamanians during Japanese occupation." On

Veterans Day 1985, the U.S. Marine Corps officials recognized Adolfo Sgambelluri for his contribution and made him an honorary staff sergeant in the Marines.

Sgambelluri's work was significant in the outcome of the trials of suspected war criminals. In a Quonset hut at the top of Nimitz Hill on Guam, the U.S. Navy War Crimes Commission on Guam put on trial 144 accused military and civilian war criminals. Of those, 136 were found guilty, including 111 who were convicted of murder. Fourteen were found guilty of torture or maltreatment of prisoners, both military and Guamanian. Two were convicted of cannibalism. Others were guilty of mutilation of the bodies of dead POWs. Sentences ranged from less than five years for some up to the death penalty for thirty-six of them. Of the latter, twenty of those found guilty had their sentences commuted to twenty years. Thirteen died by hanging. The gallows were in a different Quonset hut on the island. Most of those sentenced to prison served their terms in Sugamo Prison in Tokyo. It was there where many Japanese who were charged with spying for the Allies during the war had been executed.

When mop-up operations began after the formal end to organized resistance, the Guam Combat Patrol was organized in November 1944 to help find the hundreds—maybe thousands—of Japanese who were apparently hiding on the island and had not yet been found by the Marines or Army. There were plenty of swamps, caves, and jungles in which to hide, plus the stragglers stole and dressed themselves in GI fatigues, khaki shirts, and trousers to camouflage their appearance. The mission of the volunteer patrol was to move about on foot and question islanders in order to track and capture fugitives and blow up their hideouts. The U.S. command told the patrol members up front that this would be one of the most dangerous military combat duties yet on Guam.

The group was successful, killing about 120 Japanese and capturing five alive. But, true to the warning, it was a deadly job, too. Two members died in action when members of the patrol passed the mouth of a cave and a hail of shots rang out, cutting them down. Two others were wounded in another incident when a Japanese soldier lying on the ground and believed to be dead suddenly jumped up and hurled a grenade at them.

The patrol's leader, police staff sergeant Juan U. Aguon, received the Silver Star from President Harry S. Truman, not only for heading up the unit but also for one particular incident that vividly showed the danger of their task. It also demonstrated that the islanders were not just facing lone stragglers out there. The Silver Star citation read, in part:

"Remaining in a forward position on April 4 (1945) when his patrol was fired upon by approximately 25 enemy troops, Staff Sergeant Aguon led his men in fighting the numerically superior Japanese group, mortally wounding five of the enemy, forcing 12 over a steep cliff to probable death below and routing others into the jungles. Under his direction, the patrol then destroyed two months' provisions in the hostile camp and returned to headquarters without a casualty. By his perseverance, indomitable spirit and outstanding courage at grave personal risk, Staff Sergeant Aguon strengthened the bonds of friendship between the peoples of Guam and the United States and rendered valiant service in combating a common enemy."

As a group the patrol was awarded the Bronze Star. The unit was not formally disbanded until November 1948. One of the men, George Flores, who was wounded in the grenade-throwing incident, later said, "I take pride in saving lives, defending, and serving the people of Guam . . ."

Then he added, ". . . and for still being alive."

Another survivor among the Chamorros was Antonio Palomo, the boy who witnessed the Japanese invasion at ten years old and then the liberation by American forces when he was twelve. Obviously he was too young to help the Americans or his people at the time, but he certainly did much in later years to preserve the history of Guam. The boy who watched through his car window the nine Japanese aircraft as they bombed and strafed his island went on to get a degree in journalism from Marquette University in Wisconsin, then worked as a college instructor, journalist, and historian on his native island, maintaining a promise he had made to himself to keep the long and spirited story of his home and its people alive for future generations.

Palomo served three terms as a senator in the Guam legislature and then worked for the U.S. Department of the Interior for twelve years. Additionally, he served as presiding officer of the First Constitutional Convention of Guam in 1969 and 1970, which reviewed the Organic Act of Guam and recommended changes to the federal law. Palomo was museum director and administrator for the Guam Museum for eleven years, continuing his efforts to preserve the story of his beloved island. A new Guam Museum, containing more than 250,000 unique artifacts, documents, and photographs in its collections, is named after him.

Palomo died in February 2013 at the age of eighty-one and was buried at Pigo Catholic Cemetery in Agaña.

One person whose story Antonio Palomo helped to make known was that of Catholic priest Father Jesus Baza Dueñas. It was he who was conducting the solemn portion of the festival at Dulce Nombre de Maria Cathedral-Basilica when the Japanese roared in and began bombing the island. He was only the second Chamorro to be ordained as a priest and had to tend to his flock during its most difficult time, during the occupation by the Japanese. Dueñas was born on the island in 1911 and, at the age of fifteen, left Guam to attend the San Jose Seminary in Manila. He was ordained in 1938 at the Agaña cathedral, the first such celebration of its type on Guam.

When the Japanese invaded the island, the peaceful priest put together a group of men around his hometown of Inarajan, on the southeastern coast, to attempt to resist. As did the Marines and his island's formal forces, they realized the futility of the effort and laid down their weapons. When all American missionaries and ministers were rounded up and exiled, two Chamorro priests, Dueñas and newly ordained Father Oscar Calvo, were reluctantly allowed to remain on the island. There was a reason. The Japanese were afraid relations with Guam residents would get even more testy if they took away the two Chamorro priests. And they needed the local people to do much of the work of preparing the island for defense against any possible retaking by the Americans.

Of course, the occupation forces kept a close eye on both men. They constantly shadowed Father Dueñas wherever he went, and they threatened many times to exile him. Even so, he often counseled the locals not to cooperate and did what he could to openly question the cruelty of the Japanese, boldly standing up against injustices when he saw or heard about them. He often took his complaints directly to the occupation officials. They still considered him as little more than a significant nuisance, but necessary to keep the Chamorros under control. Even when Father Dueñas would quietly hum American songs in public or sit in the plaza and read an American magazine, just to get under their skin. And even when he was accused of spreading the news of the American victory over the Japanese on Saipan. Dueñas knew who on the island had clandestine radio receivers, including, early on, George Tweed, and helped keep the Chamorros updated on the news around the world.

In late 1942 the Catholic bishop in Japan informed Father Dueñas that he was to be appointed temporary head of the church on Guam. But the bishop was going to send two Japanese priests to "assist" him. Dueñas was certain these newcomers were agents of the Empire of Japan, especially when the new arrivals went about the island making speeches, lauding the benefits of the island now being a part of the Empire. They were always in the company of Japanese military officials, though, causing some to wonder if the new priests were making the speeches because they believed what they were saying or because they were forced to.

But one thing during the occupation finally got Father Dueñas in serious trouble with the Japanese. That was the enemy's continued concern about the whereabouts of radioman George Tweed. It is surprising it took so long, considering all the rewards offered and all the physical intimidation the occupiers were meting out, but inevitably rumors began that the priest knew Tweed's hiding place. That other Chamorros had shared with him what they knew about him. Those rumors finally got Dueñas arrested on July 8, 1944.

He was jailed, beaten, and tortured for days. So was his nephew, Edwardo Dueñas, often in the same room and at the same time in hopes one would talk to save the other. The Japanese demanded that the men reveal where Tweed was hiding and give them the names of anyone who was assisting the fugitive sailor. It was true that the priest knew a great deal about the whereabouts of Tweed and the other five sailors as well as the identities of those who harbored them and provided them with food, medicine, and shelter. He also knew of the plans of search parties and patrols that were sent out looking for them, and there are reports he often managed to get that information to the fugitive American sailors.

However, despite the brutality of their interrogation, neither Dueñas gave the Japanese any information. Bruised and bloodied, the two men were taken to the headquarters of the Japanese military police for even more brutal interrogation.

A Chamorro who was working there offered to help them escape while their guards were sleeping, but the priest refused. He maintained he had done nothing wrong and God would look after him. Dueñas also knew that if they fled, the Japanese would likely go after his and his nephew's families, as well as anyone suspected of helping them get away.

On July 12, nine days before American Marines would come

ashore to begin the liberation of the island, Father Dueñas and his nephew, along with two other Chamorro men, were taken to a Japanese agricultural field station. All four men were beheaded.

Throughout the four-day ordeal, the priest reportedly told the men torturing him that he "answered only to God, and the Japanese are not God."

In March of 1945, an interpreter from Tinian who had witnessed the execution of the four men took Father Calvo, who survived the occupation, to the crude grave where Dueñas had been buried. The body was moved to his parish church, St. Joseph's, in Inarajan. Later, a school was established bearing his name near the location of his murder. Since 1970, July 12 has been designated as "Father Dueñas Day" on Guam.

One of the miracles of the two battles for Guam involves another "survivor," one of huge importance to the people of the island. That was the statue of the island's patron saint, Our Lady of Camarin—also known as Santa Marian Kamalen and "Mary of the Crabs." Just after the first Japanese bombs rained down on the island, interrupting the Feast of the Immaculate Conception and sending children and other celebrants running in panic, Father Dueñas gathered up all the valuable artifacts of the Dulce Nombre de Maria Cathedral-Basilica. He hauled them to the home of the Torres family in the village of Maite, overlooking the cliffs west of Agaña. There he prayed they would be safe from the bombs and the Japanese invaders. And that prayer especially applied to the ancient wood-and-ivory statue of Mary.

ONLY THE BRAVE

Legend says the artifact had ended up on Guam when a Spanish galleon was shipwrecked nearby in the year 1620. According to the story, it was found by a fisherman in the sand, mysteriously surrounded by crabs and burning votive candles. Regardless its origin, though, the statue meant much to the Chamorros and everyone else on the island, Catholic or not, and not just on festival day.

It fell to a teenager, Mariquita "Tita" Torres, to care for the image during the occupation. The Japanese had issued an order that all missing artifacts must be returned to the church, where, it was assumed, they would be destroyed. One day, soldiers followed Father Dueñas to the Torres home. While there, they noticed the statue standing in the corner of the living room. Tita bravely resisted, maintaining that it belonged to the Torres family, not the church, and that they only allowed the church to borrow it for occasional celebrations. Father Dueñas lied and backed up the young girl's story. The Japanese soldiers, obviously unfamiliar with one of the strongest legends associated with Guam, decided to allow the icon to remain there, at least for the time being.

After that close call, the family moved to their ranch near Tiyan, in the Barrigada hills area. They took with them Our Lady of Camarin as well as other items from the church. When the American bombing campaign started, and when artillery shells from both sides fell all around the Torres ranch, Tia made certain the statue was moved to a bomb shelter in the rocks near their ranch. Amazingly, no bomb found it. Nor did the Japanese ever locate it again, take it, and destroy it.

The statue was enshrined back at the church—which had

also somehow managed to survive serious damage when almost every structure around the Plaza de España had been obliterated—on December 8, 1945.

That was the first observance of the Feast of the Immaculate Conception since the day war had come to the island exactly four years before. And Mary of the Crabs became yet another miraculous survivor of both of the battles of Guam.

CHAPTER FOURTEEN

PROMISES KEPT

Shoichi Yokoi was a twenty-five-year-old conscript in the Imperial Japanese Army in 1941 when he made a sacred promise to his ancestors, his country, and its emperor. He vowed to die rather than allow himself to be captured alive. Ultimately, and to his admitted shame, he was unable to keep that pledge.

Although he was shipped to the island of Guam in February 1943 and assigned to the IJA garrison defending the island, it would be almost twenty-eight years later before he would leave the Marianas and return to Japan. He had spent the entire time hiding in the jungles, rocks, and caves on the island, evading American Marines, the Guam Combat Patrol, and average citizens who still searched for Japanese soldiers like Yokoi who might still remain.

Initially, he and nine other stragglers avoided capture by the Americans by moving from one hideout to another. The others, one by one or in small groups, were either captured, were killed, or died of hunger or disease. But Yokoi kept going, eventually settling in a more or less permanent spot along the Talofofo Creek in the island's southeast sector.

There were others who managed to avoid capture on the island for many years after its liberation. Two of the Guam escapees were captured within days of each other, in May of 1960. Local islanders were harvesting breadfruit one day when they came upon IJA private Bunzo Minagawa. He and a fellow Japanese soldier, Sergeant Masashi Ito, had also gone into hiding in the last days of the American assault. The authorities were able to get Minagawa to convince Ito that it would be best to surrender, that the war was long over. Both men reported that their commanders told the troops before the assault that the Americans would treat them brutally if they surrendered, including torturing them.

That resulted in a wretched sixteen years of existence for the two soldiers, including constant fear of being captured. As Minagawa later told reporters, "We ate roots, worms, grass and grasshoppers . . . You can't imagine such a life. We were sleeping every night in the rain on the ground."

The worst part for them, as it was for Yokoi, was that they were often within sight of civilization, of people once again happily going about their daily lives while these soldiers were separated from home and family and struggling to stay alive and undetected. Early on, U.S. aircraft dropped Japanese-language leaflets over the jungles informing stragglers that the war had ended, that relatives were anxious to know if they were still alive, that it was safe to give themselves up. Ito, Minagawa, and Yokoi each reported that they did not believe what the leaflets claimed, that it was merely propaganda.

Later, neither Ito nor Minagawa admitted to knowing of Yokoi's existence, even though they hid most of the time in the same general area of the island.

It was January 1972 when fishermen Jesus Dueñas and Manuel Garcia went out hunting one day. They had no idea they would bag a legend—the last remaining Japanese soldier on Guam. They spotted Yokoi as he checked one of his fish traps he had set in the creek. At first, because of his small stature, they thought he was a local boy they knew. But when he realized he had been seen, Yokoi charged the hunters. The two men were able to easily overcome the fierce but emaciated soldier. They took him to Agaña, to the police, but stopped on the way at the home of one of the men to allow Yokoi to eat a bowl of soup.

When authorities later inspected Yokoi's cave, they found an armed bomb, along with handmade tools, animal traps, and weapons that were far too rusty to be of use. Yokoi had called on his tailoring skills to make clothing from stolen burlap bags, coconuts, and plant fibers from the jungle.

Later, at a press conference hosted by the island's governor, Carlos Camacho, Yokoi told of keeping himself clean by bathing in the creek and felt that was how he was able to avoid the illnesses and infections that had claimed other Japanese stragglers after the battle. The soldier was somewhat taken aback when he suddenly became an international celebrity, especially in Japan, where he was hailed as a hero.

He told a reporter, through an interpreter, "I wish I did not cause so much trouble to everyone. I should have just stayed in my cave until I died."

Although he said he did know of fellow stragglers Ito and Minagawa, he did want to pay respects to two others, Shichi Mikio, a soldier, and Nakabata Satow, a civilian worker, both of whom had survived into the 1960s but had died when they ate poisonous plants and toads. That came after a typhoon wracked Guam and it was especially difficult to scavenge for food.

The loyal Japanese soldier was returned to his home country in February 1972. One of the first things he said upon arriving at the airport in Tokyo was, "It is with much embarrassment that I return." Yokoi also told journalists, "I am deeply ashamed at my failure to serve His Majesty."

A month after his arrival back home, he celebrated his fifty-seventh birthday.

Yokoi admitted that he had been aware that the war was over, and realized that Japan had lost, way back in the 1950s. But he still remained in hiding. For a long time he feared he would be killed immediately by the Chamorros, who he knew had suffered so much. Or that he would be treated harshly by the military should he be captured. But the primary reason he remained in hiding was out of loyalty. He added, "We Japanese soldiers were told to prefer death to the disgrace of getting captured alive."

When the media frenzy subsided, Shoichi Yokoi eventually married and settled down near his boyhood home in rural Aichi Prefecture. He later became a television personality, lectured often on the benefits of austere living, wrote his autobiography, and was the subject of a biography and a documentary film.

The Japanese government awarded Yokoi as back pay a lump sum the equivalent of $300 in American currency. He also received a small military pension.

He never had the opportunity to meet the emperor to whom he had been so loyal, but on one occasion, while visiting the Imperial Palace in Tokyo, Yokoi continued to apologize for what he saw as a failure. He sent word to Hirohito, saying, "I deeply regret that I could not serve you well. The world has certainly changed, but my determination to serve you will never change."

A heart attack did what war and twenty-eight years in hiding in the jungles of Guam could not. Shoichi Yokoi died in 1997 at the age of eighty-two. He was buried near Nagoya, beneath a gravestone his mother had purchased back in 1955, shortly after the Japanese military informed her that her son had been officially declared dead.

Just as Yokoi had kept a promise to his emperor, another "straggler," George Ray Tweed, kept his own vow, one that he had made to a friend on Guam. After missing by eleven days the long-awaited landing of U.S. troops on the island where he had hidden from the enemy, the Navy kept Tweed plenty busy. He heard news of the successful invasion while listening to a radio in San Diego. He expressed his hope that some of the information he had been able to share had helped in the effort. After seemingly endless debriefings by intelligence officers, he was assigned to visit war plants all around the country for what were termed "incentive" talks, spurring the workers on to produce more tanks, planes, and bombs.

All the while, Tweed reported that he was worried about the many people on Guam who had been of such help to him during the time he was hiding from the Japanese. And especially Antonio and Josefa Artero and their children. After hearing rumors of atrocities and mass executions of Chamorros during the American siege, he became even more concerned. He even wrote a letter to Major General Henry Larsen, the island commander, asking if there was any word on their situation. When there was no reply, Tweed assumed the news was not good.

Then, from nowhere, came a new assignment for Tweed. The Navy wanted him to go back to Guam and do his incentive speech for the troops helping rebuild the devastated island. And while there he could also locate and learn the condition of those people he was so worried about.

When Tweed's aircraft approached the previously familiar island in September 1944, he could hardly locate most of the towns from the air. That included Agaña and Sumay. He did learn about the fate of some of those who had aided him, although many were still afraid to speak to him or talk of what had happened while they had been under Japanese occupation. There were simply too many enemy troops remaining on the island for them to feel comfortable yet. What news he did get was mixed.

One man, Juan Pangalinan, had been brought in for questioning shortly after Tweed's escape from the island and just before the American assault. He specifically was picked up because the enemy had gotten information that he had been in contact with the fugitive American sailor. Pangalinan had actually been of great help to Tweed, but he never admitted it. He had no way of knowing at the time that Tweed had already been rescued. After being viciously tortured, he finally admitted having seen the radioman a few times without reporting it to the Japanese. He was tied to a tree and put to death.

Tweed also learned that the enemy had sent word to Antonio Artero at one point, ordering him to come in with his family for questioning, even as the American bombing and shelling continued each day. Despite the imminent invasion, the Japanese were still trying to locate George Tweed. And that was when the Artero family had fled to Tweed's old cave in the ravine on the mountaintop from which they began their torturous existence until the Americans finally came and rescued them.

Those were some of the stories Antonio Artero shared with Tweed once they reunited. And Artero insisted that George spend time with his family at the ranch while he was there. The Navy was reluctant. Americans, and especially those in uniform, were subject to attack by the Japanese still on Guam. Even two months after the official end of the battle, the Marines and the Guam Combat Patrol were still killing about thirty-five Japanese each night. It was dangerous to move about. The Navy finally relented, however, and allowed Tweed to make the Artero ranch his headquarters during his stay.

One of the first things Tweed wanted to do was visit his old hiding place. The Marines were reluctant, afraid enemy stragglers might have moved in. But he finally got permission to make the trip anyway. He found it pretty much as he had left it before the Navy destroyer picked him up near the base of the cliff. There were no signs the stragglers had made use of it yet.

At the end of the visit, and as he again looked out his airplane window at the northern shoreline of Guam, Tweed reflected on his time there. He later wrote, "I know that island now. I knew that land from having crawled over it on hands and knees. I understand the Chamorros, having seen them suffer. And I knew that these people were as brave and loyal as any who ever lived under the American flag."

But that was not Tweed's final trip back to Guam. During long conversations in that dark cave with his friend and protector, Tweed had continually asked Antonio Artero what he could one day do for him to show his appreciation for the many risks he had taken. For jeopardizing his life to help the Navy man. For taking food from his own family to make sure Tweed did not go hungry.

Artero had mostly refused to even discuss such a thing. Finally, after much prodding, the rancher and merchant admitted he would like to have a newer car. His old one hardly ran anymore. The war, the loss of livestock on the ranch, and the destruction of his meat market in Agaña had left him too broke to buy one. Tweed promised he would see what he could do if he ever made it home alive.

After that September 1944 visit to Guam, Tweed decided he had to do something for his friend. It was time to keep that promise. Without expecting much, he started by going straight to the top at General Motors, writing a letter to the president of the company, explaining who he was, what had happened, and what he had in mind. As it turns out, the executive had heard about Tweed through the media and he was happy to help. The situation would become a promotion to highlight the resumption of auto production for the civilian marketplace after the war. He would donate a car, a 1946 Chevrolet just off the assembly line, but it would be up to Tweed to find a way to get it across the Pacific Ocean, all the way to the Marianas.

That proved to be no big issue, either. The Navy agreed to ship the automobile. And in 1946, George Tweed was able to keep his promise to an old friend.

It should be noted that when Tweed returned to Guam with the automobile for Antonio Artero, he learned that some of the islanders were angry with him. They resented reports by some that he had, while hiding in the jungle, taken unnecessary risks that had gravely endangered those who were helping him. And that some Chamorros had been tortured and even killed because Tweed was on the loose. Some felt he should have given himself up rather than put so many islanders at risk. Still more were upset that when he came back on the previous visit after the battle, he did not try to find many of the others who had assisted him early in his isolation. Tweed later stated that he did attempt to find them, but the island was still in a state of chaos, he had only two weeks to be there, and he had simply not been able to track down more of them to thank them personally.

The radioman had also published a book by then about his experiences on Guam. Tweed did not write the book himself. It was based on interviews with Tweed conducted by author Blake Clark. Tweed claims to have never read the full work but told many people that he had to continually ask Clark not to fictionalize some aspects of his story. The book did make what some considered negative statements about the two highly revered Catholic priests on the island, Father Dueñas and Father Calvo. Tweed later disclaimed those portions of the book and apologized for unintentionally allowing them to be included.

George Tweed never changed his attitude about one thing. That was his dislike for the Japanese. In a newspaper interview in 1987—forty-three years after the end of his ordeal—he was asked by a reporter from the *Pacific Daily News*, based on Guam, if he would ever consider returning to the island one more time. He answered he most certainly would not, primarily because of all the Japanese tourists he would inevitably see there.

Tweed told the reporter, "If I should meet any of those Japs on Guam, I would just spit in their faces and probably get in a lot of trouble. I still remember how much they enjoyed killing and slaughtering the Chamorro people."

The little girl whose family helped hide him on Guam would later relate to reporters what she felt was the primary reason so many Chamorros risked their lives to help Tweed. Carmen Artero—later Carmen Artero Kasperbauer—recalled, "Tweed was the American symbol our parents fought for and some died for."

She went on to tell a reporter, "Our parents did what they did because of their love and belief in God and their love for America. The Japanese tortured and killed our people because of our love and belief in America and protecting an innocent person against an enemy."

Tweed did maintain a close friendship with the Artero

family. Antonio and Josefa visited him several times at Tweed's home in Oregon. However, true to his word, Tweed never did return to Guam after that trip to deliver the car. And some on the island who are still alive dispute some of the other actions and events Tweed described in his book, which he had titled *Robinson Crusoe, USN.*

The Arteros remained friends with Tweed regardless of what may or may not have happened during the years Artero helped hide him. They had kept their own promise to keep him safe from the Japanese. They also remained loyal to the United States despite what many Chamorros and family members felt was gross mistreatment of him by the U.S. military after the war.

Because of the island's newly appreciated strategic and tactical location, the U.S. Air Force ultimately decided to build a major air base on Guam. It was to be named North Field. Much of the land on which the base was to be constructed belonged to the Artero family, as it had for many generations. However, the U.S. government forced Artero to sell it to them at what many believed to be an unfair price. They did allow him to retain one narrow strip of land but forbade any development of the property because of its proximity to the new base. He would even be required to ask for permission from the military officials to visit his remaining acreage.

Today, that facility is Andersen Air Force Base, considered by most to be the most important air base west of Hawaii. That is primarily because of its ability to host in that part of the world heavy strategic bombers, such as the B-1B, the B-2, and the B-52, as well as several types of spy aircraft. Its proximity to China and North Korea has only increased its value.

President Harry Truman made Antonio Artero one of the first to receive the Medal of Freedom in 1945 (now the Presidential Medal of Freedom), primarily for his efforts on Tweed's behalf. Truman established the award specifically to honor civilian contributions to the victory in World War II.

Artero never gave up his determination to get at least some of his family's land back. He was unable to do so. He always maintained that he was proud of what he did during the war and deeply honored to have received the Medal of Freedom, but he would have preferred the return of some of the land he always felt was virtually stolen from him. Artero even wrangled an appointment with President Ronald Reagan, which he hoped was an opportunity to make his plea. Reagan was scheduled to stop over in Guam while on his way to a state visit to China, but Artero was too ill to make the meeting with the president. He died in May 1984 at the age of seventy-nine.

George Tweed received the Legion of Merit and Silver Star and was promoted several times, first to the rank of chief petty officer, then warrant officer. He finally retired from the Navy in 1948 with the rank of lieutenant. In civilian life he opened a television repair shop in Los Angeles and later moved to Oregon to fix TVs and run a dairy farm.

His story became the basis in 1962 for a motion picture entitled *No Man Is an Island*. Tweed was played by the actor Jeffry Hunter. Guamanians were disappointed that the film was shot not on their island but instead in the Philippines. And that the actors spoke the Tagalog language rather than Chamorro. Tweed also appeared in an episode of the television quiz show *To Tell the Truth* in October 1962. Two of the show's four panelists correctly identified him as the real George Tweed.

Tweed died in an auto accident in 1989 at the age of eighty-six and is buried at Eagle Point National Cemetery near Medford, Oregon.

Captain George McMillin, the man who had promised to defend the island of Guam from any attack, felt he had done all he could to do just that. As previously noted, he even told a reporter who interviewed him in a Japanese POW camp to be sure to let President Roosevelt know that he and his men had tried their best.

McMillin's wife, Annabel, did receive several letters from her husband during his years as a POW, but they contained little information about his condition or location. She had been busy while her husband was held by the enemy. She had seen their daughter and son through high school and into college. And she had twice been called upon to christen new Navy vessels. The first was the large cruiser USS *Guam* (CB-2) in Camden, New Jersey, in November 1943, then the USS *American Victory*, a cargo ship designated as a "Victory ship," launched in May 1945 in Los Angeles, California.

On August 20, 1945, Soviet forces informed George McMillin and other prisoners at the Mukden, Manchuria, camp that the war was over. They were free. Once back home, he continued his career in the U.S. Navy until his retirement in June 1949. He left the Navy with a rank of rear admiral and later became the postmaster of the U.S. Post Office in Long Beach, California, where he served for eight years.

McMillin died in August 1983 at the age of ninety-three.

Private First Class Ray Church, one of the young Marines who vowed to defend the Government House and the island of Guam against insurmountable Japanese forces early in the morning of December 10, 1941, also spent the rest of World War II in prisoner-of-war camps on the Empire's Home Islands. In 1943 he was taken from his first camp to a different and even worse one. There, he would later recall, the only thing he had to eat was warehouse sweepings. He had to pick out individual grains of rice from rodent waste, straw, and bugs just to survive.

In 1945, Church was working long days on a dock in Osaka, sleeping in filthy barracks nearby. One night the Americans bombed those barracks and he was burned when he was splashed by napalm. The incendiary liquid had been developed after the start of the war and was, by then, being used in the massive fire-bombing of Japan's major cities; many of the planes involved originated from the Marianas. Another prisoner managed to put out the flames and likely saved Church's life.

Ray Church later recounted a day just like any other but for one thing. Nobody appeared before daylight to awaken the POWs and herd them to the docks for the day's labor. Nobody. Their Japanese guards simply did not show up. A few days later, still with nobody coming to get them, they learned from civilians that the war was over. Thankfully, those civilians shared food and water with them until the Americans were finally liberated. For Ray Church, it had been more than forty months of brutal imprisonment, starvation, beatings, and forced labor.

Later, when he was asked how he was able to survive such harsh treatment, Church said it was because he and his fellow prisoners were all in the same boat. They spent time talking about their experiences in life so far and helped keep one another's morale as high as possible. He also said he had a great deal of pride in being an American and did not want to let his country down by giving up.

After getting back to the States and spending time recuperating in a naval hospital in San Diego, Church finally went home to Utah. There he opened and ran a movie theater, then moved to Los Angeles, where he spent forty years in the banking industry. But he admitted that the first ten years after the war were difficult, as he suffered from bad dreams and monumental sadness.

Church went back to Guam once and laid a wreath at a memorial for U.S. soldiers, sailors, and Marines who died in the war. He also visited the National World War II Memorial in Washington, D.C. Church passed away in January 2013 at the age of ninety-two, at the George E. Wahlen Ogden Veterans Home in Ogden, Utah. He is buried in the Delta City Cemetery in his boyhood hometown of Delta, Utah.

Another POW who survived his time in the Japanese camps was the sailor Edward Howard, who helped scuttle the "Old Duck," the minesweeper *Penguin*, and was assisting the Marines in digging in to protect Guam when the war started. Of course, Howard had some added incentive to protect the island: he had married a Chamorro woman and they had two children, including a girl born only days before the Japanese attack on

Guam. That meant that, unlike other American servicemen whose families had been evacuated, all three of Howard's dependents were on Guam when the invasion happened.

Once he became a prisoner, Howard's wife, Mariquita, had managed at great risk to smuggle a Bible to him. While enduring brutal treatment over the ensuing years, he would read from the Bible to other prisoners. Howard was in constant fear he would be beaten or killed if the Bible were found. But one Japanese soldier, a camp translator who was secretly a Christian, allowed him to conduct funeral services for men who died and to read from the book. Howard would later talk of how that Bible and his own faith helped him and others survive inhumane treatment at the hands of the Japanese.

One of his guards once told Howard, "It is Japan's aim to give its prisoners of war as much pain as humanity will allow." It seemed to Howard that humanity was allowing the Japanese quite a lot.

After the war, in a book on his experiences, Howard wrote, "The Japanese considered people who surrendered to be cowards and beneath contempt, and they treated their prisoners that way." For most of his more than four years in the various camps, he and his fellow POWs unloaded coal, bauxite, iron ore, and scrap metal from ships, usually with little food or protection from the elements. In his book he wrote, "We were given the equivalent of four slices of bread for lunch. We were given a teacup of rice morning and night, along with a cup of hot water that was called soup, the kind of stuff that is discarded before vegetables are taken to be sold." They were often beaten or forced to stand at attention with their arms raised. Anyone who moved was punched. Sometimes, for no reason, they were ordered to stand in a row and count off in Japanese. Any prisoner who made a mistake was punished.

After being freed at the end of the war, Howard learned his wife had been killed by the Japanese when she refused to have sex with an officer. Though still weak and sick, he went back to Guam as soon as he could to get his children and try to locate his wife's remains. He never found the spot where the Japanese buried her.

Howard reenlisted in the Navy and eventually remarried, this time to a woman who had two children from a previous marriage. But tragedy struck again: his second wife died in an automobile accident. Howard would spend many years suffering from what is now known to be post-traumatic stress disorder. He once wrote, "I do believe that the (deceased) POWs that I watched being burned in the furnace in Japan were the lucky ones." Later in life, he became active in helping develop new ways of treating PTSD. He did get his college degree and served as a library administrator.

Ed Howard passed away in 1990 at the age of seventy and is buried in a military cemetery near Marion, Indiana.

Lieutenant Colonel William MacNulty, the commander of the Marine contingent on Guam in December 1941, was also a prisoner of war for the duration of the conflict. The recipient of the Navy Cross and the Silver Star for gallantry in the Nicaraguan campaign, in the so-called Banana Wars, and in the Argonne Forest in World War I—obviously a valuable warrior—found himself sidelined from the war's first day to its last. But his contributions were not ignored. He was promoted to the rank of brigadier general in 1942, even as he was a POW, performing forced labor far away from his native Pennsylvania.

Later, General MacNulty expressed pride in how his Marines had performed against overwhelming enemy forces during the attack on and invasion of Guam. He retired from military service in 1946 and died in 1964 at the age of seventy-two.

Most of the senior commanders in charge of Operation Forager, the recapture of Guam and the rest of the Mariana Islands, went on to long, distinguished careers.

The hero of the decisive battles of Midway and the Philippine Sea, Admiral Raymond A. Spruance, who oversaw Operation Forager, went on to succeed Fleet Admiral Chester Nimitz as commander in chief, U.S. Pacific Fleet—Pacific Ocean Areas, in November 1945. After the war, the Navy had a limit on the number of five-star admirals they could appoint at any one time. Spruance never received the rank, but by a special act of Congress, and to show appreciation for his stellar service, he was awarded equivalent admiral's pay for life. President Truman later appointed him as U.S. ambassador to the Philippines.

Spruance died in Pebble Beach, California, in December 1969. He was buried at Golden Gate National Cemetery in San Francisco as part of a unique "band of brothers" arrangement. In addition to his wife, buried alongside Spruance are Fleet Admiral Chester Nimitz, Admiral Kelly Turner, and Admiral Charles Lockwood, all naval heroes of World War II in the Pacific and longtime friends. The men had concocted the unique eternal plan long before their deaths.

Two destroyers were named *Spruance* in his honor (DD-963 and DDG-111). The main auditorium at the U.S. Naval War

College in Newport, Rhode Island, is named Spruance Hall. There is a bust of the admiral in the building's lobby.

Vice Admiral Kelly Turner, the man directly in charge of the forces bent on retaking Guam, retired from active duty in July 1947 and passed away in Monterey, California, in February 1961. He is one of those buried alongside Nimitz, Spruance, and Lockwood at Golden Gate National Cemetery.

The destroyer USS *Richmond K. Turner* (DLG-20/CG-20) was named in his honor. Turner appeared in the 1945 documentary film *To the Shores of Iwo Jima* and was portrayed by the actor Stuart Randall in the 1960 film *The Gallant Hours*, about Navy admiral William "Bull" Halsey.

Major General Roy S. Geiger, the former enlisted-man private and early Marine pilot, went on to see even more action after leading his amphibious forces ashore on Guam. He would even be commander of an Army unit. After capturing Guam, he led the assault on Palau later in 1944 and took more troops ashore on Okinawa in June 1945. This time his Marine unit was part of the Tenth Army. During bitter fighting on Okinawa, Lieutenant General Simon Bolivar Buckner, the commander of the Tenth Army, was killed in action. Roy Geiger assumed command for the final five days of the battle. That, so far as historians have been able to determine, is the only time that a Marine has been in command of a field U.S. Army unit. Another claim to fame? Despite the massive contribution by Marines in the war in the Pacific, General Roy Geiger was the only Marine Corps representative present at the surrender of Japan aboard the USS *Missouri* in Tokyo Bay in September 1945.

Geiger died in January 1947 at Bethesda Naval Hospital in

Maryland. The former private was promoted posthumously to the rank of four-star general by the Eightieth Congress. He is buried at Arlington National Cemetery.

Medal of Honor recipient PFC Leonard Mason was twenty-four years old when he died defending his fellow Marines from machine-gun nests on Guam on W-Day plus one. When he enlisted in the Marines in April 1943, Mason took an oath and made the same solemn promise as his fellow Medal of Honor recipients Frank Witek, Luther Skaggs Jr., and Louis Wilson, did: "I, _____, do solemnly swear that I will support and defend the Constitution of the United States against all enemies, foreign and domestic; that I will bear true faith and allegiance to the same; and that I will obey the orders of the President of the United States and the orders of the officers appointed over me, according to regulations and the Uniform Code of Military Justice. So help me God." (An officer's oath is worded slightly differently.)

Secretary of the Navy James V. Forrestal presented the Medal of Honor posthumously to PFC Mason's mother, Mollie Partin, with two of his sisters looking on. The young Marine had been buried at sea.

The destroyer USS *Leonard F. Mason* (DD-852) was christened in his honor in 1946. Then, in 2013, Middlesboro, Kentucky, the town where he was born, renamed a stretch of one of its primary streets, Cumberland Avenue, as Leonard F. Mason Medal of Honor Memorial Highway.

Marine PFC Frank Witek was twenty-two years old on August 3, 1944, the day his platoon was ambushed. The day he refused to dive to the ground as the others had done but instead remained standing, shooting into a hole filled with enemy troops to give his buddies the opportunity to find cover. Who stayed behind to guard a fallen platoon member, then provide cover fire for the wounded Marine and his stretcher-bearers until they could get clear. And who again charged a Japanese machine-gun emplacement that threatened to decimate his platoon, losing his life in the process.

On a Sunday afternoon in May 1945, more than 50,000 people gathered in Soldier Field in Chicago to see Private Witek's mother, Nora, receive her son's Medal of Honor posthumously. He was initially buried in the Army, Navy and Marine Corps Cemetery on Guam but was reinterred in 1949 at the Rock Island National Cemetery in Rock Island, Illinois.

The destroyer USS *Witek* (DD-848) was launched in 1946, christened by his mother.

Although Witek grew up in Chicago, his birthplace was Derby, Connecticut. In 1999 the town named PFC Frank P. Witek Park in his honor. Guam named a facility near Yona as Marine Camp Witek, and although the camp is no longer open to the public, area residents still refer to the area as Camp Witek. The Marine Corps Scholarship Foundation continues to award a scholarship in honor of PFC Witek.

Luther Skaggs received his Medal of Honor personally from President Harry S. Truman in a ceremony at the White House in June of 1945. Several reporters took note of the fact that the number "3" had played a significant role in his story. He had been born on the third day of the third month of 1923. When he went ashore at the Asan-Adelup Beachhead on the island of Guam, he was a part of the 3rd Battalion of the 3rd Division of the 3rd Marines.

Eleven days after the White House event, Skaggs went home to Henderson, Kentucky, for even more honors. That trip was almost canceled because of the possibility of more surgery on the leg that had been shattered when a Japanese grenade rolled down a cliff and into his foxhole. But he made it back for what the local newspaper described as the biggest parade in the history of Henderson, "including two tanks, a half-track, an armored car, and miscellaneous other vehicles—followed by a company of WACS."

When it came time for him to address the crowd, Skaggs said, "I did the best I could."

The "uncomplaining and calm" Marine was later promoted to the rank of corporal and discharged honorably on April 4, 1946. He died thirty years later, almost to the day, on April 6, 1976, and is buried in Section 46 of Arlington National Cemetery in Washington, D.C.

After being wounded three times in a running, raging ten-hour battle on Fonte Plateau in July 1944, Captain Louis Wilson was evacuated to the U.S. Navy Hospital in San Diego, California, for treatment of his serious injuries. But this would not be the last war for him. As it turned out, the young officer from Mississippi was just beginning a long and distinguished career in the Marine Corps and he would be vitally involved in several more conflicts.

As with PFC Luther Skaggs, Wilson received his Medal of Honor personally from President Truman, but only after he was assigned to become commandant of the Marine Barracks in Washington, D.C. After being promoted to the rank of major and then lieutenant colonel, he served with the 1st Marine Division in Korea. Later, he held key command positions with the 1st Marines in Vietnam, where he received the Legion of Merit award and the Republic of Vietnam Cross of Gallantry with Gold Star. He eventually earned two more Legion of Merit awards.

Wilson was promoted to general in July 1975 and assumed the position of commandant of the Marine Corps at an especially crucial time for that branch of service. After Vietnam, it had become difficult to recruit qualified people to the Corps, but Wilson insisted on raising standards, increasing training and readiness, modernizing the Marines, and restoring consistency. He would also be the first Marine Corps commandant to serve as a member of the Joint Chiefs of Staff.

Wilson retired in June 1979 and died in June of 2005. He was buried with full military honors at Arlington National Cemetery. Louis Wilson Drive in his hometown of Brandon, Mississippi, as well as Wilson Boulevard and Wilson Gate at Camp Lejeune, North Carolina, are named in his honor. So is Wilson Hall, headquarters building for the Marine Corps Officer Candidates School in Quantico, Virginia. The *Arleigh Burke*–class destroyer USS *Louis H. Wilson Jr.* (DDG-126)—under construction at Bath Iron Works in Maine as of this writing and scheduled for completion in 2023—is named for Wilson.

Promises made and kept, these four Marines certainly epitomized the spirit with which the Americans returned to reclaim the island of Guam and her sisters in the Marianas.

Not all promises have been kept, though. To this day, many on the island are of the opinion that the United States still owes much to the land where its day begins.

Carmen Artero Kasperbauer would ultimately sum up well the painful, conflicted thoughts of so many of the Chamorros who were fortunate enough to have survived the war. As a young girl, she saw firsthand the horrors of both battles, the atrocities committed by the Japanese during their occupation, and the bloody, destructive consequences of the liberation. It was during the joyous festival of Santa Marian Kamalen at her church that she first experienced the sudden panic as she witnessed the Japanese air attacks on her peaceful island. She worried, suffered, and sacrificed so her father could help feed and conceal George Tweed. Happy as she was to be set free by the American Marines from the cave where she and her family were hidden, where her mother was at the point of death, she still lamented the brutal results of war on her family, her home, and her people.

"To me, it is no different from someone being physically or sexually abused," she would later tell an interviewer. "You feel as if your soul has been invaded. It is wrong for two powerful nations to war on such a small island. And afterwards, the two nations made amends between themselves but never made amends to us. I feel we are not thought of as real people and afforded our equal rights, our citizenship. We are only Americans at the whim of the federal government. I feel this injustice has to be corrected."

However, she did not stop there. "But I want to say, we love America. We love Americans."

Then, through tears, Kasperbauer concluded the interview with a thought shared by so many once they have experienced the horrors of war.

"And I pray that someday love, peace and justice will come from all this."

★ AUTHOR'S NOTE ★

As an author, I have written and published nine books so far dealing with World War II. All but one are set in the Pacific theater. However, I admit that I knew little about Guam and the part it played in the war. I understood the battle was part of the Marianas campaign but not much more. On the time line, I knew it fell somewhere after Guadalcanal and before Iwo Jima and the Philippines. I did not know why the Marianas were so critical to the war effort, nor was I aware of the size of the assaults on Saipan and Guam, or that Guam alone involved almost 80,000 troops and resulted in the deaths of more than 20,000 of them.

I also admit to not even being aware that there were two battles for Guam. And I certainly did not know of all the very personal human stories that came from those two conflicts, especially those involving the Chamorro people, who had occupied the island for about 4,000 years. Their suffering and sacrifice during the war, caught in the crossfire between Japan and the Allies through no fault of their own, is one of the most powerful and poignant I have heard. Especially when we consider that as a people and island, they have "belonged" to someone else—Spain, the United States, Japan, and the United States again—for five hundred years.

Theirs are the kinds of stories I enjoy relating, as well as those of the men on both sides of the conflict: admirals and generals, privates and corporals, and everyone in between—flesh-and-blood stories of seemingly ordinary people who were placed in unusual situations and then did remarkable things. That is why I am grateful to my literary agent and my editor for giving me the opportunity to learn more and then relate their stories. Hopefully, many others will not be as uninformed as I was. They will know what happened, where, and who did it.

In the process of researching and writing this book, I have once again been surprised at how even the most thoroughly studied and documented events are susceptible to errors. I work especially hard to avoid them, but even seemingly impeccable sources will have varying "facts," spellings, dates, or other significant differences among them. This is even true of those who were there or deeply involved in such events and tried to relate them accurately. In a work such as this, almost every sentence requires research and verification. I have tried to be as accurate as possible, since any error calls into question everything else in the book.

I do especially appreciate accounts and documentation that

appear to have been thoroughly researched and accurate based on hours of cross-referencing. This has been a challenge here because so little has been compiled on the battles of Guam. I have relied on several helpful works and oral history collections that have assisted me in telling the story, often from the perspectives of people who were there.

Readers who may desire to dig deeper—especially those who seek far more detail about particular battles, strategies, tactics, specific military units involved, and the like—may certainly take advantage of these research sources that have proven valuable to me in my effort to tell a much more human story exactly the way it happened.

One is Gordon L. Rottman's *Guam 1941 & 1944: Loss and Reconquest* (Oxford, UK: Osprey Publishing, 2004). It is a detailed schematic of the battles from a military perspective, and the edition I used featured excellent maps and reproductions of paintings that aided my understanding of time and place. I have relied in the past on other books in this series from the same publisher and they have each been helpful.

Another primary source is a truly remarkable monograph now reproduced on the internet and titled "Liberation: Marines in the Recapture of Guam" by Cyril J. O'Brien (1994). This document was published for the education and training of Marines by the History and Museums Division, Headquarters, U.S. Marine Corps, as part of the fiftieth anniversary of the end of World War II. It is available online (as of this writing) at http://www.ibiblio.org/hyperwar/USMC/USMC-C-Guam/index.html. Note that O'Brien was a Marine sergeant who was there during the Second Battle of Guam.

A third key source, and one also available on the internet, was a series of articles published to commemorate the fiftieth anniversary of Guam's liberation day. It was produced by the publications subcommittee of the Guam Golden Salute Committee and edited by Antonio (Tony) Palomo and Paul J. Borja. The compilation was titled "Liberation—Guam Remembers: A Golden Salute for the 50th Anniversary of the Liberation of Guam." It is currently available for viewing on the National Park Service's website at https://www.nps.gov/parkhistory/online_books/npswapa/extcontent/lib/index.htm.

Another detailed work dealing with the Second Battle of Guam concentrates on the participation of and contributions by the U.S. Army 77th Division and its role in the conflict. It is titled *Guam: Operations of the 77th Division—21 July-10 August 1944*, compiled and published by the Center of Military History, United States Army, Washington, D.C., after first being researched and published by the Historical Division, War Department, for the American Forces in Action series in 1946.

Yet another valuable source was a video compilation of oral histories by Chamorros who were on Guam during both battles, recounting their own personal experiences. Titled *An Island Invaded—Guam in World War II*, the film was produced by Pacific Resources for Education and Learning, a 501(c)(3) organization, and funded by the U.S. Department of Education. It is currently available for viewing on YouTube.

The book *Robinson Crusoe, USN* by George Tweed, Blake Clark, and Alan Anderson (originally written in December 1944 and published by Whittlesey House in 1945, reissued as a self-published work, date unknown), was a primary source for information about Tweed's exile on Guam in the midst of enemy troops for thirty-one months. As noted in my recounting, the accuracy of some material in the book has been questioned, including in annotations added by Anderson in later editions. I have used only those elements I believe to be accurate and confirmed by other sources. That meant I had to omit some very interesting material.

Segments of oral histories were captured from a number of sources, including the University of Texas at Austin's Voces Oral History Center; the Legacy Series in the Oral History Program at the Museum of History and Holocaust Education at Kennesaw State University in Kennesaw and Marietta, Georgia; the Earwitness to History project at the Library of Congress; the online oral history resources of the National World War II Museum in New Orleans, Louisiana (especially the recollections of PFC Ray Church); and the Stamford Historical Society's Pride and Patriotism: Stamford's Role in World War II online collection.

Other books that offered source material and served as confirmation of information found in other sources include:

The Pictorial History of Guam: Liberation 1944 by Don A. Farrell (Micronesia Productions, 1984)

Marines in World War II: The Recapture of Guam by Major O. R. Lodge (Verdun Press, 2014)

Saipan and Guam: The Official Marine Corps History of the Marianas Battles of World War Two, U.S. Marine Corps Historical Branch (2015)

Captured: The Forgotten Men of Guam by Roger Mansell and Linda Goetz Holmes (Naval Institute Press, 2012)

Bundschu Ridge: At the Tip of the Spear During the Liberation of Guam by Scott W. Carmichael (self-published, 2014)

God Shared My Foxholes: The Authorized Memoirs of a World War II Combat Marine on Bougainville, Guam, and Iwo Jima by PFC Joseph Friedman, Retired (iUniverse, 2010)

Finally, I would like to thank the proud Chamorro people of Guam for maintaining the legacy of their ancestors by preserving their stories and experiences. As a storyteller who aims to keep this kind of eyewitness history alive, I continue to encourage people to capture oral history by any means they have and then make sure it is available for historians, writers, and others. This is the only way to assure that they and their experiences are never forgotten and makes possible a much better understanding of historical events from a uniquely human perspective.

I maintain a website, Untold Millions: The Oral History Project, to encourage collecting memories of those who have not only fought wars but who were instrumental in the civil rights struggle, in the development of the space program and the computer age, and more. And from all levels, too, from cook or ditchdigger to admiral or president.

We have buried or cremated millions of untold stories of those who have been eyewitnesses to history.

The website is available at www.untoldmillions.net.